From the
Mating Dance
To the
Cosmic Dance

From the
Mating Dance
To the
Cosmic Dance

SEX, LOVE, AND MARRIAGE FROM A YOGIC PERSPECTIVE

Swami Sivananda Radha

Timeless Books

publishers of timeless wisdom

TIMELESS BOOKS
PO Box 3543
Spokane, WA 99220
1-800-251-9273 • www.timeless.org

In Canada: Timeless Books, Box 9, Kootenay Bay, B.C. V0B 1X0
- (604) 227-9224

In England: Timeless Books, 7 Roper Rd., Canterbury, Kent
CT2 7EH - (0227) 768813

Printed in the United States of America

Cover and interior illustrations by Deborah Pohorski
Cover and interior design by Ian MacKenzie

Library of Congress Cataloging-in-Publication Data:
    Sivananda Radha, Swami, 1911-
        From the mating dance to the cosmic dance : sex,
    love, and marriage from a yogic viewpoint / Swami
    Sivananda Radha.
            p. cm.
        Includes bibliographical references and index.
        ISBN 0-931454-31-X (hard) : $22.95.
        ISBN 0-931454-32-8 (ppk.) : $14.95
        1. Yoga. 2. Sex--Religious aspects. 3. Marriage--
    Religious aspects. 4. Love--Religious aspects. 5. Spiritual
    life.
    I. Title.
    BL 1238.36.S58   1992
    294.5'44--dc20   92-13848
                                          CIP

It is my prayer that the tools offered here will help all women and men who are suffering injustices in their lives to find their own inner Light.

Contents

Acknowledgments

MANY PEOPLE AND EVENTS over the years have contributed to the writing and production of this book.

My Guru, Swami Sivananda, was an exceptional teacher of Eastern philosophy, but he was also unusual in the support he gave to women for obtaining education and gaining self-respect. I had the opportunity to witness him encourage women to accept promotion and to believe in themselves.

When I first started to put teaching material together, Rita Foran was a very patient note-taker. We used an old technique for the first book we worked on—making long scrolls by cutting and sticking together pieces cut from typewritten material. Now Rita Foran is using modern equipment—Apple computers. In other ways she has also taken another step in her own life and development by becoming Swami Padmananda and functioning today as the president of Yasodhara Ashram.

It may not be known to many people that the name of the Ashram was given by English settlers in 1887, which is also the birth year of my Guru. I knew that Yasodhara was a woman. In fact, she was the Buddha's wife, and as Yasoda she was Lord Krishna's foster mother. So when I learned the name that had been given to the property, I knew beyond doubt that the Ashram should be dedicated to helping women come into their own.

That was accepted by Deborah Pohorski, whom I encouraged to put the gist of the poetry into a drawing. That is creativity at its best.

Ian MacKenzie traveled the road from student to teacher. He passionately taped instructions and every talk at satsang, and, in a whirlwind of activity, put them onto the computer. In this way the copy editor/designer was born.

Karin Lenman, a professional editor, made her way to the Ashram as a seeker of the Most High, and she offered her services. She, too, very quickly could grasp the deeper meanings of the material.

Linda Anne Seville worked for one of the biggest oil companies when I first met her, and she was wondering what kind of position she could achieve among executives who were all men. She was very effective in promoting my lectures, and, recognizing her talent, I suggested that she consider a total change, and take on what was then a fledgling publishing company started by students who wanted to have the Teachings in print.

I wondered what men would say to a book that was, to a large degree, guidance for women. What would be the response particularly from those who are academically trained? When the first draft of the manuscript came to physicist Tom Weaver, his response was so positive that more material was included to deal with the struggle that modern men face.

And what about the scholars of Eastern teachings? The claim is usually made that women do not have enough understanding. Not so John Grimes—an advaita vedantin and in the department of religious studies at Lethbridge University—who was very enthusiastic. He understood the different practical way I had chosen to help people so that the scholarly works could become tools in the daily lives of those who seek the Most High.

To all of them my heartfelt thanks.

Foreword

WHEN SCIENTISTS HAVE INVESTIGATED the nature of the external world, they have found again and again that the story of the universe is the story of evolution—evolution from a *single* concentrated form of force and energy to a diverse cosmos full of myriad worlds and life forms. The current scientific understanding of nature is now deeply rooted in the idea that nothing is in essence different from anything else: seemingly different particles and forces (from electrons to quarks, from gravity to electricity) are thought to be like different facets of the same "crystal." The interplay of this one basic force with itself has seemingly given rise to the wondrous diversity that we now experience.

But evocative though it may be in understanding the "how's" of the natural world, science can even now offer no fundamental understanding of the nature of consciousness: the nature of the inner world of awareness that we all share. Questions concerning the meaning and purpose of life (not to mention experiences like joy and wonder and love) are simply beyond its scope. For millennia saints and sages, and, to some extent, each of us, have instead looked *inside* to try to find the answers to these questions. In doing so, we come face to face with the many "longings" that inhabit this world: the longing to survive, to grow, to procreate, to gratify our emotions and senses, to love, to control, to be free, and ultimately to find union with something greater than our individual selves.

Is it possible that all these longings are interrelated aspects of one central driving force? The urge of consciousness to evolve and its potential to become more manifest? This is the statement that Swami Radha makes based on her many years of practice and teaching of Yoga—the ancient practical science of the exploration of consciousness. In particular, she challenges us to cooperate with our own evolution: to climb the ladder from mechanical patterns, emotional gratification, and attachments, to cultivating refined feelings, becoming aware of our actions and motivations, and taking responsibility for them. She warns us that this evolution will proceed in any case, but that it will be much slower and more painful if we *choose* not to cooperate.

The focus of this book is on the roles that love, sex, and marriage play in the evolution of consciousness. Many books have been written on the nature of the mating dance, as well as spiritual treatises that immediately go "beyond all that" to the lofty heights of Cosmic Love and Unity. The great value of this book is that it deals with these themes in a way that is concrete, explicit, and direct, while keeping the underlying spiritual issues in perspective. The result is very different from a manual of "Thou shalts" and "Thou shalt nots," or, on the other hand, a license to "go with the flow." It is, instead, a set of tools, ideas, alternatives, and questions aimed at helping us loosen up and clarify our preconceived ideas and habitual patterns of behavior in these areas. For example, Swami Radha asks us to examine in detail the image of our "Dream Lover" and to consider the consequences of trying to view another person through such a filter. At each stage she shows us practical ways to bring quality and awareness into our relationships with our spouses, partners, and families.

A central theme is that each of us has the power and responsibility of choice in how to use our creative energy, and that, with growing awareness, these choices (and responsibilities) expand. She makes it clear that love, sex, and marriage are not distracting side issues to spiritual development, but involve basic energy, interactions, and conflicts that both test and nurture our developing awareness. They provide a concrete way of putting our spiritual ideals into practice. Her promise is that each time we choose to exercise our powers of discrimination, intuition, and compassion, and to examine the results of our actions with fierce honesty, that our consciousness will expand, and that even our mistakes will be stepping-stones.

The final chapters of this book describe how the mating dance evolves into the cosmic dance of spiritual unity of the individual self with the power of consciousness that underlies and pervades our inner and outer worlds. Perhaps such a possibility should not be too surprising, even to a scientist. The underlying interconnection and unity of the physical world, despite its evolution into myriad forms and forces, suggest that the evolution and nature of consciousness may be no different. In the end, however, this issue will be settled, not by speculation, but—as this book stresses—by the personal experience of all of us in following the path of the evolution of awareness, and seeing where it leads.

THOMAS A. WEAVER, Ph.D.
Department of Physics
Lawrence Livermore National Laboratory
University of California

Great wisdom in disguise
of an awesome serpent,
crushing illusions, childish plays.
Power of immensity
turning into a dragon
guarding the entrance
of the hidden place.

A Word from the Author

THE PURPOSE OF THIS BOOK is to help you fulfill the purpose of your life. I wrote it to give you the tools that I have, so that you can help yourself solve your problems.

It became impossible for me to personally answer all the letters I received, and it was also impossible for everyone to make the trip to Yasodhara Ashram in western Canada. Whatever their struggle, people hoped that there was a greater purpose in life. They questioned why things needed to happen in the dramatic, cruel way they do.

My personal life experience, my ups and downs, the struggles with my own problems, and even my dreams, have given me the understanding and the tools I am now passing on. I was only three years old when the First World War broke out, and as a five- and six-year-old I had to flee from snipers on my way to school. My family, like many others, lost everything in the war. Then came the Depression, and then the Second World War. During that war I even had to take the dead bodies of their babies from the arms of mothers who could not accept death. The facts of life are cruel, but although I might put a pink ribbon on them, the cruelty does not disappear.

In the West we think that the dramas of life occur as payment for our sins, but my Guru, Swami Sivananda of Rishikesh, has said, "We all learn by trial and error." So I give you the philosophy of the East, from wherever I have gathered it: I stayed in various Eastern monasteries, and traveled as well in the Middle East, to find out about the problems people have to face in different parts of the world. I found that human beings are the same the world over. We must all meet challenges to move ahead on the path of evolution, and we must all learn to accept those challenges. History tells us that all achievements have been won through trial and error, and by accepting the challenges presented, until something was established on which another generation could build.

If we are unwilling to make the changes that our challenges demand of us, then we are being perfectionist. Perfectionism does have a certain place in our life, but we must realize that true perfection is found only in the divine Self. Nothing else is perfect. The fact that we have an idea of perfection, that we even have the word in our vocabulary, is probably because we intuitively know where that idea comes from, and all of us would like to have that perfect relationship within our divided self. We have a physical body that is tangible, and walks on the earth. We have a spiritual body, a divine body that is invisible to us. It lives in a very different realm. When we are in the human realm, we long for the spiritual realm and experience an almost painful loneliness. When we are in the spiritual realm, we are full of compassion for the human realm. To unite them takes tremendous effort. We play many games to attain what we want in life, but this is the Master Game—the desire for the Most High nourished with great intensity. If we want to be on the spiritual path we must play this Game because, although we may not be winners, it is our only chance to become true masters of ourselves and our destiny.

There is a question that is often asked by people who are in search of greater awareness, Higher Consciousness, and Liberation: How do we live our daily life?

I have to tell you that it is no easy matter. The problem is that you want too many things; you want to have your cake and eat it, too. When we have too many diversions, we cannot give ourselves wholeheartedly to any one thing. For instance, if you are in a marriage relationship, then either your husband or your wife comes first, and the Divine takes second place.

The couple who will both pursue a spiritual path is very rare, not even one in a thousand. Emotional needs, and the obligations and habits from old traditions all interfere. Despite your best intentions, the effects of tradition alone can prevent you from carrying out your intent. We seldom recognize the hypnotic effect of tradition and conditioning in our life, and we seldom think deeply enough to discover the source of these ideas, and the control they have over us. In this book I have tried to stimulate your interest to do your own reading and thinking about the source of concepts that you hold.

There is no tradition in the West to help a husband and wife follow a spiritual path together. Yet I have found over and over again that couples who have drifted apart can only be brought together by giving them a spiritual ideal to move toward independently and separately. In that way, they come together slowly and with understanding, until they eventually meet at the top of an ascending triangle.

Is it possible to achieve a wonderful marriage? It is, but you have to work at it, as you have to work at any other achievement in life. You have to meet yourself on the gut level and see things as they are, not as you would like them to be. The challenges offer you the opportunities to grow, to recognize what are facts, what is wishful thinking, what are illusions, and what are dreams.

A husband and wife on the spiritual path who have been married for years, and are not planning to have a child, are at least taking responsibility for their actions. But we cannot speak in the same breath about the average couple and the one that seeks Higher Consciousness. We cannot compare a piano teacher in a village with somebody who is training to become a concert pianist. It is not *bad* to be a village piano teacher, but it is not enough if you want to become a concert pianist.

This book is to help people who practice Yoga, who want to have awareness, and are willing to pay the price.

A famous violinist was once asked, "You don't practice anymore, do you?"

He said, "Yes, for four or five hours a day. Previously it was six to eight hours a day."

"Do you have a family?"

"Yes."

"Do you still have time for your wife?"

"No."

If you want to become a genius in your field, then you cannot apply the same criteria to your life as would someone on the street.

In order to have more yogis and yoginis in the world, we need parents who are willing to bring up their children with that purpose in mind. When a child is an unwanted by-product of the parents' pleasure, then sex is bad, because another human being is involved, whose life will be miserable from day one. How could I say that sex is fine when that happens?

Some people must follow their instincts because that is where they are anchored and where they want to remain. We have reduced sex to a level where it has little meaning, and where there is no commitment to one another. Even when there have been enough problems and crises to make people stop and ask themselves, "What's life really all about?" they still want to have their cake and eat it, too.

For ordinary people who are married and have children, this book will help them to investigate their values: "Can I see clearly? Is it enough for me to be a good music teacher, or do I want to be center-stage?" They can decide. But then they cannot ask, "Why haven't I achieved Realization?"

People have said to me, "I have done this and this and this. Why don't I have Realization?" It is because that is not where their minds were.

How far do you want to go in Yoga? Do you just want to become a better person, a more aware person? That's fine. You decide how far you want to go. But don't fool yourself into believing that you can have the highest consciousness while living a very ordinary life, that you can become a great violinist without needing to practice many hours a day. Just to play in an orchestra you have to be good, and that means daily practice at home. It's very nice to come home, have a glass of wine with your husband or wife, look at the sleeping children, and maybe look forward to having another baby. But then there is no practice, and when the marvelous position does become available, you cannot make it because there are many people who are so much better, who gave their energy to the music and becoming a top musician.

If you cry about your lost opportunities, I can shake you up and tell you to be strong. You may not like it, but it will help you to stand on your own feet and see the years you have wasted, so you can decide to do something about your life.

It is very difficult for people, especially young people, to break away from their romantic ideas, because the love affairs they see on television show the man as always good-looking, always with a car and a wonderful apartment, while the woman is always shown beautiful and glamorous. Young people take these things for real life. As long as they are happy with their life as it is, until something happens to make them think, there is no point in my telling them how to achieve Realization. If a young woman wants only to be accepted by a man as a sexual being, that is all she will be, because most men do not care for much more. If she is beautiful, then she is like a decoration on his lapel. Many people—men and women—will deny that because it is too harsh for them to accept that it is perhaps the way they are themselves. But that does not make it untrue.

I have been invited to speak at many churches and monasteries. The subject of sex, love, and marriage always comes up. How can these things be put together with spiritual life? At one time a local minister said to me, "I have a meeting with some teenagers. They will probably be happy to ask you about how they can look toward life in the future."

Of course, almost within the first five minutes they wanted to talk about sex and sexual relationships. So I said, "You know, this is not the most important thing in life. You were not born just to have sex. Let's find out what your interests are. What do *you* like to do, what do *you* like to do, and what do *you* like to do?"

So I asked everybody, and one young man said, "Oh, my favorite activity is playing Spanish guitar, but I don't have a classical guitar yet."

I said, "Well, if you were to buy one, what would it cost?"

He gave me a price, and it was a lot of money.

Then there was a very lovely young girl and she said, "Yes, I have thought about guitar, but everybody plays guitar. I play piano."

I said, "What would be your dream?"

She replied enthusiastically, "Well, can you imagine a grand piano?"

I said, "How about a baby grand? Would that do?"

"Oh, any grand will do!"

This was precisely where I wanted the young people to be. The
essence of that meeting was that I said to the young man, "Do you
leave your Spanish guitar in the backyard?"

He looked at me as if I must be stupid. What a question to ask!

"And would you let your little brother run his toy automobiles
over the smooth surface of your baby grand?"

Now this girl really had to control herself. She was about to tell
me that I was mad. It was very obvious on their faces, but that was
precisely where I wanted them to be. That is why I had made those
remarks. I said, "Look, you can always buy another Spanish guitar,
and you can always earn the money again for a baby grand piano. But
you can't buy another body. Why would you not want to treat your
body with the same care and attention as your musical instruments?"
After that we didn't need to talk about sex any more.

If you don't value your human body, and cannot see this body as
a miracle in itself, why should you experience a different kind of
miracle? You would not even understand it, because your senses are
too gross. They are not refined.

If your relationship with your partner is not sacred, and the offspring that come from that relationship are not well received, are not
wanted, and are not brought up for the glory of the Most High, what
is your life? You are living like cats and dogs. They have their young,
too. The difference for us as thinking beings is what we do with our
consciousness, and we must start with these little ones, by not talking
down to them, but helping them to think differently. The new generation must bring quality into life. Otherwise why should this earth
continue to exist? Why do you think that the threat of global disaster
hangs over people's heads? If life is not precious, if life is not sacred,
and if parents don't teach children the sacredness of life, then why

should it be? These are the questions you will have to ask yourself. This is where you begin to think how to bring quality into your life.

An old master, who wanted to explain to his disciples that Realization cannot be given to those who do not want it, brought some beautiful Chinese silk to show them. He held it up so that they saw only the back, and he said, "How do you like this?"

They said, "Oh, it's great. It's wonderful!"

Then he asked them, "Have you seen it?"

"Well, you are holding it up. You are showing it to us."

"But have you seen it?"

They wondered.

"What if you could have more?" Then he turned the piece of silk around, and there was a big sigh in the room. He said, "This is what you *can* get. So don't be satisfied just with the partial picture, just with what gives you a little of the design and the color of what spiritual life or Divine Union *can* be."

Even the greatest love affair in the world comes to an end, if in no other way, then finally by physical death. If you have a love affair with the Divine, when you leave this earth it is really only *beginning*. So why be satisfied with less, if you can have so much more?

What I have to tell you is very practical, and if it can help you to improve yourself, your life, and your relationships, I will be most happy, because I will have succeeded in my purpose.

Consciousness is without sex.
Something is latent—not lost
in recesses of the mind (memory).
Smoldering ashes still glow
to light a lamp—to find the way.
Even a small flame overcomes
darkness.
Light is not enough.
Action must follow . . .
climbing the path.

1 Evolution

EACH CULTURE sees human life as a progression through a series of stages. These systems may have been developed in an attempt to understand the evolution of human beings and the vast differences in human intelligence. The search for an explanation might have begun with an exploration of the five senses, with the ability to think and interpret evolving out of that exploration and becoming the sixth stage, and the longing to go beyond it all creating the seventh.

We see this evolution in the seven chakras of the Kundalini system,[1] which indicates most clearly the process of human development, because it is the culmination and combination of all paths. We see it as well in the seven rungs of Jacob's Ladder[2] in the Judeo–Christian tradition.

The levels of human development are also symbolized by the Buddhist Wheel of Life,[3] concentric circles arranged according to the goal in life. Those people on the outer circle are just holding onto life; for them it is a matter of survival. Each one of us has to move through many lifetimes, from the outer circle to those circles within. At the very central point of the Wheel is the Buddha of Infinite Light, the point that is completely motionless, balanced. All of these systems—yogic, Christian, or Buddhist—can be used as frameworks for learning discrimination, with each level or circle representing a further refinement of our power to discriminate.

The Inner Light, Buddhahood, Christ-Consciousness, Nirvana, as specific stages of the mind, are often used as the central point or goal of human endeavor and development.

These ideas from the past are continued in present-day life when we measure our potential as levels on intelligence tests. But even the particular phase of life we are in is an indicator of development, because we have achieved that phase through the choices we have made, and those choices depend on the discrimination we have practiced—our level of awareness.

It is commonly accepted that certain preliminaries must be fulfilled in order to achieve specific goals. For example, the baby does not need to know the multiplication tables or to recognize the root of a word in Latin or in Greek, nor is it expected to be able to walk a tightrope or perform physical gymnastics. But there are very definite expectations of the understanding, behavior, and training at that stage. Moreover, what takes place in the first few years of life has a tremendous impact in later years and can be crucial to the possibility of developing further.

We speak of the infant, the toddler, the preschooler, the kindergarten child, and the elementary school student. These various stages are accepted as a logical progression. If we consider human potential and its development in the same light, we see that the powers and qualities we can achieve also evolve through similar stages. Whenever we enter a new phase or learn a new skill, we can detect these same stages, although we may move through each of them very rapidly. The newcomer to physics feels as ignorant and helpless as a baby. To become an astronomer or a physicist, one must possess a certain level of ability in mathematics; to become a composer or conductor one must have perfect pitch, then develop the ability to read music and play an instrument.

Ernest Wood, in his book *Practical Yoga: Ancient and Modern*,[4] has given us a fresh approach to the ancient concepts of developmental levels, to help us understand the stages we already perceive in life. He uses five stages to demonstrate the evolution of human consciousness, and the powers that can be developed in each, the last being the full realization of one's potential. I have added a sixth to indicate the potential that is promised by Yoga: the emergence of the enlightened being.

The six stages form convenient divisions to help us understand the complexities of human nature, but this does not mean that people are categorized exclusively into any one of these divisions. In fact, we never function on one level only, but on several at the same time. However, in order to assess more clearly the problems that cause us pain, and to point the way to solutions that will lead to a more enlightened way of being, it is necessary to distinguish between the various stages.

Ernest Wood has named each of these stages.[5] The first stage is Mineral-Man, representing people who live by their instincts, with little desire to achieve a different position or increase their knowledge. At this stage we want nothing more than to gratify our basic appetites for food, shelter, and sex. Intelligence is at its lowest, so our limited ability to learn and remember makes it impossible to attain precision in skills or to broaden our understanding, often to the point where we are even unable to recognize the possibility that we can improve. At this level we lack reverence for life and appreciation of beauty in art or nature. We lack initiative and take no responsibility for our actions.

The second stage is named Vegetable-Man, also an apt description. Large numbers of people live like vegetables, although perhaps a better term is *weeds,* which push into any cultivated garden, destroying it if they are left unchecked. We can recognize in ourselves the greed for self-satisfaction that pushes everything else out of its way. Greed is the motivation for people primarily in the mineral and vegetable stages of development. Initiative and creativity are still dormant, and self-gratification is so dominant that if any finer forces are awakened, they are nipped in the bud by the prevailing greed and self-importance.

Animal-Man, the next stage, is more aware of ego and its games. In this phase we add cunning to our vegetable pushiness, so we become more clever in controlling others, with little regard for their right to dignity. Although we have not yet fully developed an appreciation for finer expressions of creativity, we make a pretense of being interested. However, simply being exposed to a creative atmosphere allows a slow entry of this dimension into our lives.

In their ignorance about life and themselves there is a certain innocence about people in the stages of Mineral- and Vegetable-Man. They grab things without awareness of what they might destroy in the process; they may even take delight in the destruction just for the pleasure of destroying. But as our awareness increases at these levels, destruction becomes a conscious, intentional act and it is ugly. No longer is hunting limited to obtaining food for survival; it becomes an ugly act of killing for its own sake.

When pleasure enters into killing, it does not stop short of killing human beings. People who live mainly at the level of Animal-Man increase their abuse of power in all areas. Their cleverness masks itself as wisdom, covering the ugliness ever more skillfully. Their urge to control comes in many disguises. Their intention to exploit increases like a gathering wave.

To someone at the level of Animal-Man, sex is no longer just a biological function as it is for those at the mineral or vegetable stage; sex now is used primarily for pleasure. Instinctual biological functioning is Mother Earth's trap to continue her numerous species. Many forms of birth control have been devised to avoid the possibility of pregnancy, and so prevent interference in our pursuit of pleasure. Our desire for convenience and our reluctance to take responsibility for unwanted offspring then trigger legal actions that expand into laws about, for example, abortion, paternity and child support. By not taking responsibility for their sexual behavior, men and women in this stage are helpless and are therefore at the mercy of those whose only love is power. That power is exercised in all areas of life, from advertising that exploits our basic instincts, to social policies that govern the family. The politics of controlling the growth of populations and their potential for exploitation is a battle in which those who are controlled hate the controllers, and the controllers hate those they control.

We can think of life as a schoolhouse, with the lowest grades having the greatest number of students. As the learning process continues, the numbers become fewer and fewer, because the problems become increasingly complex. Similarly, the greatest number of people in our society are still mainly in the first three levels of development and, although we may smile sardonically at primitive people for creating gods and goddesses with the hope that they will fulfill their desires, we do the same thing.

We can see that clearly in our society's emphasis on food and sex. We often use sex for purely physical gratification, as an expression of personal power, and for punishment and reward. And although we recognize that its purpose is procreation, we strongly battle this intention of nature. Our attempts to circumvent any obstacle to our sexual gratification have led us to serve our own gods and goddesses of power.

In the first three stages, we learn from the challenges presented to us by the activities and responsibilities of sex, love, marriage, family, and children, and apply in our lives what we have learned, just like students passing their grades in school. But the high price in pain and disappointment that comes from the gratification of self at all cost brings the dawning understanding of the futility of such pursuits. The desire for something more worthwhile comes to life within us—something that justifies the price, and we begin to ask ourselves, Why am I here?

We have searched for answers to that question in religion and science, philosophy and politics, throughout history. Our struggles in the animal stage force us to look more closely at this question, to lift our vision, expand our horizon, and finally take the daring step into the next stage, that of Man-Man. Here we are faced with the need to control instincts and to take charge of our lives. But logic is not enough, and an understanding emerges that it is through intuition that we can make the leap.

The fourth stage in life, called Man-Man, means to become truly human: we become considerate of our fellow beings, appreciate their accomplishments, and recognize that competition is an offspring of our struggle for survival. Now we can understand survival in a new light. In this stage we need new visions to provide meaning for life.

The burden of the first three stages is not easily thrown off, and the perspective of the new horizon appears so vast and overpowering that we can easily become discouraged. Our familiar ways are still attractive. We may feel the agony of being close to something that is struggling to emerge from the depths of our inner being, yet is held back by an indefinable fear.

At this level we begin to apply discrimination rigorously. We begin to question the origin of the morals of our culture, how they have come about, whether they are indeed just taboos of the past, or if they still have validity. Ethics, responsibility, and commitment versus the pursuit of purely personal pleasure come under our scrutiny. What we had previously considered right becomes more and more questionable when we enter the fourth stage.

As we consider new viewpoints, the question arises whether we should or can change our attitudes toward sex. Can sex become a transforming power that elevates us into a different state of awareness? Does our search for higher values require self-mastery and control of sexual urges? On this level we might for the first time consider such an idea as celibacy or chastity, or we may look for a more fulfilling sexual relationship, one that now includes love. At this point, we ask ourselves for the first time what love means to us.

Sexual love implies a different quality of interaction, and perhaps a new dimension is added to what had been simple, raw instinct. As we cultivate ourselves and slowly move along the path of evolution, some laws of the first three stages no longer apply, or they change drastically.

In human history, the concept of love emerged slowly from the world of purely sensory experience.[6] The idea of love could come only after our longing for more than gratification directed our vision beyond the merely physical experience. Out of this longing arose both the Christian concept of altruistic love (agape) which made a great impact on ways of thinking and living in the Western world, and the Eastern teachings that demand self-mastery, control of the basic sex urge, and the ability to forego greed and to renounce self-will. When these principles are applied to our lives, a new atmosphere is then created in which love can unfold, and allow us to transcend the lower levels of being.

From a yogic point of view, when we become truly human our awakening to the purpose and higher values in life shows that we understand, perhaps only intellectually at first, the relationship between individual consciousness and Cosmic Consciousness. With this increasing awareness, our ability to accept responsibility expands because we more fully understand our personal path of evolution.

People are at many different stages of development. But the only real difference between them is that some know they are divine, and others do not yet have that awareness. In many lifetimes each one of us has gone through the lower forms of evolution, and in each lifetime we have refined ourselves. We have participated in the course of evolution as we understood it and were capable of carrying it out. Now, at this level of becoming truly human, we can choose not to be controlled by the lower instincts, and our sexual expression assumes different qualities, as does all of life. But we must remember that there is an interplay of the forces within us. We never function on one level only, but on several at the same time. For example, there is an interplay of the senses at all times: we never only see, but at the same time we also hear, feel, taste, and smell. So we cannot always expect ourselves to be operating only on the highest level.

Our increasing awareness and development bring the realization that pursuing the goal of Higher Consciousness carries with it a certain obligation. Once we eat from the Tree of Knowledge, we have responsibility. At this point we must decide whether or not our desire for Higher Consciousness is so pressing that we must pursue it at all cost.

It is difficult to change human nature until we have achieved the first degrees of awareness, of becoming truly human. The changes involved entail suffering for a time, but the suffering that results from greed, selfishness, and self-glorification is unending and undiminishing. Character-building, therefore, is the necessary first step. In the yogic tradition, the next step is to ask the important question, What is the purpose of my life?

After the fourth stage of human nature, we approach the fifth stage of the spiritual being: God-Man. Here we know that our search for higher values and spiritual development is cooperation with our own evolution. The thought may now enter our mind that the purpose of life is not orgasm. Awareness of the fleeting nature of this experience brings pain, because we realize we truly are alone. But at the same time, we recognize that we have always been alone. The busy bee of the mind with its continuous hum never allowed us to recognize that fact before. We begin to understand, too, that our purpose, as dwellers in both the spiritual and the physical realms, is to move beyond the animal aspects of the physical and to find our way to Higher Consciousness.

At the level of God-Man we want to bring children into the world consciously: not as a by-product of sexual pleasure, but as individuals whose steps we can guide toward a glorification of divine life. This is the stage at which we recognize that we are a bridge between two worlds—the physical material world and the spiritual world—and we have consciousness that is itself a power, a vortex of energy that is indestructible. Our hunger for acclaim is replaced by a hunger for true knowledge, as our search for the Light begins, our search for the essence within.

Through an intense process of thought and discrimination, at this level we have elevated the marriage relationship, and now we aim for the mystical marriage. And with the intuitive understanding that ahead there lies a greater union of the individual consciousness with God-consciousness, we realize that the physical expression of sex might not be essential. There is no suppression and there is no struggle because we have laid our foundation. Even in certain tantric systems, which do make use of the sex force, there is no seeking for personal gratification, but a surrender to whatever form in which the sexual energy might be expressed.

At this stage we begin to have an intuition of a paradise lost. We begin to understand that this physical existence is not our proper home. In each religion we find stories that attempt to answer the primary question of why we are here and why Paradise was lost. In Christianity there is the story of the fallen angels.[7] One of the Eastern

stories tells of how, at one time, there was a great fire on the earth.[8]
The waters came, putting out the fire, and the young gods in mid-
heaven, watching the drama below, said, "Now that earth is normal
again, let us go and see what it is like." So the young gods descended
to the earth plane. Some came and went, but others stayed too long
on the earth and were trapped by their curiosity. Their fine and ethe-
real bodies became so condensed and hardened that they could not
return to the mid-heavens.

The other gods of mid-heaven who came back for them said,
"Because of what you are doing, you cannot come back. Your bodies
have grown too heavy."

So the earthbound young gods became worried and said to one
another, "If our bodies grow heavy, they will die like the bodies of all
the other animals." But they saw that the animals could reproduce
themselves, and they imitated the animals in the hope that they could
reincarnate and eventually find their way home again. Perhaps we
can consider this the source of the idea of the Fall of humanity.

In Hindu mythology, Brahma created four mind-born sons.[9] The
story may be telling us symbolically that procreation can be the result
of not only physical union, but also of the power of mind over matter.
To move out of the animal kingdom, we must look at sex in a new
way. When the feeling of homesickness for our "Heavenly Home"
becomes intense, we may accept the possibility that, by freeing ourselves from the weight of habitual thinking, we can make our way
back. The practice of Yoga offers us that choice.

The Divine Union—the sixth level—can take place in many ways:
it can include the physical body and it can transcend the physical body.
The human being who reaches the sixth level of Liberated-Man, having
attained the potential promised by Yoga, provides the example for others
by following the guidelines that are set out in all Scriptures.

NOTES

[1]Kundalini Yoga is a process of evolution that, in ancient times, was pre-
served as a picture language. It is a direct path to Higher Consciousness, the

process of conscious cooperation with evolution. Kundalini Yoga has been demystified in one of my earlier books so that it can be understood and applied in the daily lives of men and women of today. See Swami Sivananda Radha, *Kundalini Yoga for the West* (Spokane, WA: Timeless Books, 1978).

[2]Elisabeth Haich, *Sexual Energy and Yoga* (New York: ASI Publishers Inc., 1976), 81–91, 155–58.

[3]See Sermey Geshe Lobsang Tharchin, *King Udrayana and the Wheel of Life* (Howell, NJ: The Mahayana and Sutra Press, 1984). The Wheel *(Bhavachakra)* is gripped tightly in the protruding teeth of a monster, whose hands and feet have nails like claws. This fierce image leaves no doubt that human beings are in the grip of many laws: the biological, the laws of nature, and also the law of action—good and bad—known as *karma.*

Around the motionless center of the Bhavachakra there are a cock, a snake, and a pig. The cock symbolizes passionate sex in its most primitive form as pro-creation and mechanical action; the snake stands for evil and temptation or, more precisely, delusion; the pig represents greed, hatred, lack of discrimination, and lack of regard for life.

The concentric circles of the Wheel with their various divisions symbolize what happens in life, beginning with the most primitive drives of human nature, and reveal the need for self-mastery. Figures of Buddhas performing spiritual acts are used to symbolize those who have achieved various levels of mastery. The ones who have achieved complete mastery can be seen as gods, whose great intellect manifests as wisdom, compassion, power, and knowledge, and in this way they represent the attainment of the highest rung on the ladder of evolution.

[4]Ernest E. Wood, *Practical Yoga: Ancient and Modern* (Hollywood: Wilshire Book Company, 1972).

[5]I have used these names given by Ernest Wood because they provide fitting descriptions for the various human stages of development. To the modern ear they might sound sexist, but please keep in mind that several decades ago when his book was written such terminology was in common use.

[6]Edward O. Wilson, *On Human Nature* (Cambridge: Harvard University Press, 1978), 86–87, 139–140.

[7]The New Testament, Book of Revelation.

John Milton, *Paradise Lost.*

[8]Swami Sivananda Radha, *Kundalini Yoga for the West* (Spokane, WA: Time-less Books, 1978), 339, excerpt from Ekottara-Agama XXXIV, Takakusu II, 737.

[9]Wendy Doniger O'Flaherty, *Hindu Myths* (London: Penguin, 1975), 50.

Gods and goddesses change
with the seasons of life.
Interest is diverted,
children being distracted,
coming of age.
Gods and goddesses expand
with consciousness.

2 *Power*

EACH CULTURE, Eastern or Western, has its own concept of what human nature is. But all cultures have in common the struggle between the physical-mental being and the spiritual being. For the person who wishes to become a spiritual being it has always been necessary to swim against the stream of life.

The part of humanity's story that is particularly pathetic and depressing is that of the countless new gods whose motivations have deteriorated with their success, leading them increasingly to attempt to control others. These gods have ranged from the tribal leaders and warriors of ancient times to today's scientists and politicians. Unfortunately, throughout history man has conquered neighboring tribes and nations, but he has not yet conquered himself, and each new group of gods to whom we have looked for leadership have not provided the example set forth in the Scriptures of all religions. Our present gods are no better.

We have made scientists our gods, and in our hope that human nature can be changed we have turned to them, and so we have spawned the study of heredity, which has led in its turn to genetic research. The result is that science is now able to fertilize ova in a test-tube, and has introduced artificial insemination, embryo transplants, artificial wombs, frozen sperm cells, the possibility of asexual cloning (or virgin birth). And now it appears that sociobiology hopes to do away with *all* problems through genetic engineering. We have become confused about the distinction between human nature, instincts, and DNA. The common saying, "It's just human nature," has found a new expression: "It's all in the genes."

However, the results that scientists achieve are simply one step in the process of investigation. And what appears to be conclusive scientific proof may even be misinterpreted, because scientists can sometimes react to experiments in a highly emotional manner when the results challenge their cherished beliefs. Emotional reactions cloud one's view, and fear prevents one from perceiving a wider spectrum.

We forget that at one time schools of thought like astrology were accorded the prestige of science, and are the basis for much of science today, even though they seem so primitive to us now. Today's science will be tomorrow's astrology, so clearly it does not have the final answers, and it is foolish to give science the power of a god.

As science discovers more and more "solutions" for the problems of human sexuality, it will become increasingly important for those of us at the mineral, vegetable, and animal stages to overcome the rulership of the instincts, to assume responsibility for our own development, and to gain freedom from the control of others. We need to remember that not one of these solutions is the final word. It is simply science's answer of the day.

We have seen many of these scientific solutions: the Pill was supposed to provide the answer for birth control; its unpleasant side effects resulted in the "morning after pill"; sterilization is recommended as freedom from unwanted offspring. These solutions had to be tested on human beings who, during that experimentation, were diminished to the animal level, because little concern was shown for their physical or psychological well-being. If scientists are to operate on the fourth level of development, they must allow their concern to emerge and ethics to come into play. Once again, in this connection, we need to raise the question, Why have we made these people into our gods?

Our hope is to achieve a potential beyond material gain. Without denying the influence of heredity and genes, the question might be asked, Who or what created the genes? Was it an independent power? Have we evolved beyond the level of our ancestors? And if so, was it because a potential existed that it was possible to develop?

The Power that is greater than ourselves cannot be reduced to a concrete level, or be made into an idol. The images we create, whether they are Father God, Earth Mother, Golden Calf, sex goddess, or the powerful in any form, are not the indestructible essence itself.

In order to achieve the clarity of mind necessary for us to develop our potential, thinking in depth with ruthless honesty is essential. But we must also practice constant awareness in order to bypass the often too-rigid intellect that easily falls into the apparent security of belief. To make these essential distinctions we need a highly refined ability to discriminate.

Modern science also tells us that virgin birth results from some quirk of nature[1] but, if to be virgin means to be untouched, pure, and of the original essence, then the need to be virgin in mind would be much more important than physical virginity. Purity of mind can be achieved only through the search for union with that Power within us, that frees us from the need to believe and to worship false gods. It is this Power that enables us to become aware of inherited attitudes that are still at the unconscious level, and to make the changes that are necessary.

The history of humanity the world over has shown a preoccupation with sex that could be called pathological. Could it be that the source of our morals and intricate taboos, in any century, at any age, is a desperate attempt at self-protection from compulsive sexual instincts? Man has divorced himself from the rest of creation just as he has from what is apparently his greatest object of desire—woman. Is it that in order to rise above his sexual greed, his compulsive need for gratification, he must protect himself with taboos just as the diabetic locks up the sugar from himself?

We see these same problems, same tendencies, same interactions in mythology: man's fierce competition with woman, and his envy of woman who can give birth to both sexes. The gods and goddesses of any religion are just one step beyond human beings, able to intervene but unable to change the essential human nature. The struggle that mortal beings undergo is only magnified in them, and shows the power of the forces that control human beings. We equate the conquering of these forces with genius or sainthood.

Dependency on woman for continuation of his own sex must have been a frightening experience for early man, when he did not know his part in creating offspring. We still scarcely understand our sex drive and our desire for continuity and immortality. According to the geneticist, any male (or conqueror) wants to propagate his own genes and is therefore very strongly attracted to healthy young females, someone else's wife, or even his own daughter. There is the biblical story that, after he had conquered the Midianites, Moses commanded that all men be killed, and every woman who had known a man. The geneticist suggests that in ordering this genocide Moses behaved in "perfect compliance with the 'central theorem' of sociobiology," and that his goal was to propagate his own genes and those of his tribe.[2]

If we accept that this action was taken in accordance with basic human nature in its early stages of evolution, we can understand the writings of Homer in the *Odyssey* or the *Iliad*, in which women lament the signs of a new war, fearing that their husbands will be killed, and they will be sold with their children into slavery. Girls sold for the pleasure of men, men mutilated and transformed into eunuchs, young girls circumcised at puberty—have these and other practices developed so that the world of sex could be entirely dominated by man, because woman seemed to control giving birth to new life?

Although the geneticist may not be absolutely correct in saying that we are merely robots controlled and manipulated by our genes,[3] there may be truth in what he says. It seems that the first three stages of human beings do indeed operate on this level. Our use of sex today is too often on the biological or pleasure level, and we have allowed ourselves to be manipulated by those in power, through our sexual drive, in the name of progress and morality. A modern example of one whom we allow to manipulate us in that way is the geneticist, whose intent is not different from Moses'. We have handed over our power to others for centuries. The primitives gave their power to the image of God they had created, or to their conquerors. Now we yield it to science. Perhaps we would do well to look to earlier cultures to help us understand the root and development of our present ideas about sex, love, and marriage.

Throughout history all social laws, rules, regulations, and taboos were man-made, and carried into the religious field. So we Westerners have inflicted our problems, our emotional struggles, and our feelings of revenge on God the Father, and we have reduced the Cosmic Intelligence to a "Heavenly Father," full of wrath and punishment, who is to be feared. This image itself stands in the way of a greater understanding.[4]

Early peoples beseeched the gods they had created to be kind, to treat them fairly, and to help them in their confused affairs. There may have been two factors influencing the emergence of this idea of an all-powerful God: first was observation of the laws of nature and the group spirit of plants and animals, as well as a group spirit of the tribe; second was the need for a leader, but of a heavenly order, a God above all other gods. But they also looked for intermediaries between themselves and their fearsome divinities, and they found them in people who had achieved an intimate connection with the Divine.

Perhaps when human awareness evolved to a point where there was the first capacity for clear thought, and when the psychological being could form ideas of consciousness, then concepts of ethics arose. It is comforting to consider that morals and ethics—beyond instincts—existed and were mirrored in the social life of the people of the past, and that today we benefit from their achievement.

We have an example in the Bible, the book that Christians consider to be the origin and foundation of their faith. Close examination of early Egyptian papyri has shown that they were the source for what became the Book of Proverbs,[5] that the wisdom of Amenemope had been translated from the papyri into Hebrew, then circulated in Palestine. So the ethics expressed in Proverbs did not originate with the Jews, but with the Egyptians 3,000 years before them. There had also been ideas of a messianic leader with no evil in his heart nearly 1500 years before the appearance of Jesus among the Hebrews, who are still waiting for their Messiah.

In any age the societal values eventually become confused, the leaders of the country are no longer benevolent, and are no longer without evil in their hearts. At such times of decadence and injustice, the undisciplined have nowhere to turn because even their belief in a benign God is shattered. But those who have disciplined themselves and practiced awareness, find in the last message of Lord Krishna both a comfort and a warning: he makes it clear that he will incarnate again and again for the sake of the righteous, to protect his own from the unrighteous. Because hope is immanent in all human life, it finds expression differently in each culture.

The waves of human development correspond to the ocean waves that surge ahead, then draw back to expose the barren sand and rock, until new forces gather to form yet another wave. Controversies arise and one philosophy or aspect of human development is rejected, but with the light of new understanding we can see that without the early ones we would not understand the ones that follow. The disputes between philosophies and schools of thought are irrelevant once we see the interaction and interpenetration of events. For example, when Jean Doresse[6] and his colleagues brought to light the Nag Hammadi manuscripts, we were given a glimpse of a little-known age that existed at the birth of Christianity, a glimpse that clearly shows the paramount importance of developing human consciousness. Through his interpretation of the scrolls, Doresse makes us aware of conflicts that developed from the influences of other races, as well as the dualistic aspects found within as the two selves, a duality linking east and west, north and south—a chain of many links strengthened by myth. These dualities meet in a center—in a crossroads—like a many-faceted diamond reflecting the Light in every direction.

New things are brought to the surface and others are lost when the wave is formed. Philosophies and religions change as emerging trends are supported or suppressed, a process we can still observe. With Christianity now so well-established, we may forget that it was based on earlier religions and that for centuries the emerging Christian sects were often disliked and forced underground.

Religion is one expression of the desire to attain our potential, but it is important to be free from dogma so that we can see the interpenetration of events, not to be believers, but to find the truth of religion, and to apply it in our lives. When a religion loses its power and enthusiastic support, our minds are prepared to receive a new belief, which in due time has to prove its right to the religious energy of its followers. Changes in religion reflect in politics: as the faces of political leaders change, they take on the status of new gods because of our inherent human need to worship.

Even with the developments in technology and science, we are still unable to free ourselves from our gods, because to do so we need clear sight and a clear mind that is devoid of attachment to beliefs. We need to apply discrimination to the claims of scientists, just as we must apply it to the edicts of religion. The god who protects his own and enslaves the wicked is mirrored in the present-day scientist who would eliminate all who came from a bad gene pool, so that the benefits achieved through genetic engineering could go to those with a desirable background.

Human beings seem to have a strong emotional need to worship success itself, regardless of how it has been gained. Conquerors who rise from the bloodshed of thousands eventually entice the ignorant to worship the power they represent. If we ponder this, it becomes clear how admirable is the struggle of the spiritual being at the sixth stage, whose life is lived against the stream of belief, social law, natural law, conditioning, and the dictates of the genes.

The search for the origin of consciousness has always been part of the path of the spiritual individual, even if it is expressed in a variety of ways. The search is open to all who are not defenders of doctrines, and are willing to escalate their ways of thinking into new ideals, who have the courage to free themselves from inherited beliefs and concepts. Ever since human beings began walking the earth, there have been enlightened people who acted with clarity, wisdom, and responsibility, even though they may have been only a few.

In our search, some very important questions arise: Since the inception of the human race, have we inherited a knowledge of higher values, or the need to search for them? And have we developed these faint inklings into gods and goddesses in order to personify consciousness? Or do the scientists imply that the animals they use in laboratories to test the new solutions for human problems, also have a sense of morals? If human beings have developed at least physically from the animal kingdom as Darwin tells us, have we inherited a basic sense of morals from the animals? Is the brain itself an organ that evolved, goaded by some inherited—if dimly perceived—idea that there is more to life than eating, drinking, sex, pleasure, and comfort? Will there be a time when every human being will be capable of using more than one-fifth of the brain? And as research on the brain and its functioning continues, will the scientist offer guidance in how to use it?

Thinking in depth and investigating our human past can help those who wish to cooperate with their own evolution. The effects of attitudes we have inherited can be seen in the interaction of men and women today, and the place that sex holds in their lives. We can use this understanding to develop ethics, ideals, and attitudes for ourselves. Awareness of human evolution will bring us the understanding that sex can be elevated from the instinctual level to the union that is the meaning of Yoga, and we will see marriage as symbolic for the Divine Union.

<hr>

NOTES

[1]David Rorvik, *In His Image: The Cloning of a Man* (Philadelphia: J. B. Lippincott & Co., 1978), 96.

[2]Alex Dorozynski, "Sociobiology: Science's Enfant Terrible," in *Science Forum Magazine* (July/August 1978), 15–16.

When Edward O. Wilson, zoologist at Harvard University, published his book *Sociobiology,* and followed later with *On Human Nature,* he unleashed fierce condemnation even among his peers. Despite clear evidence in the Old Testament of what Moses had done, Wilson has been accused of being a racist and a fascist, who uses sociobiology as a political weapon.

[3]Ibid. Dorozynski goes on to quote British ethnologist Richard Dawkins as saying, "Genes swarm in huge colonies, safe inside gigantic lumbering robots (us), sealed off from the outside world, manipulating it by remote control. They are in

you and in me; they created us body and mind; and their preservation is the ultimate rationale for our existence. We are their survival machines."

⁴The saying of Mark Twain that we were created in the image of God and have repaid that compliment ever since, has helped his readers to understand the godly human being, and the human intelligence. Plays have been developed on this theme and, while it is enjoyable to see the workings of the human mind in the setting of a theater, it is quite different to see oneself in the position of acting out a part on the stage of life, not able to get the message of the director, or to know one's entire part in the play.

⁵James Henry Breasted, *The Dawn of Conscience* (New York: Charles Scribner's Sons, 1933), xiv–xv.

⁶Jean Doresse, *Secret Books of Egyptian Gnostics* (New York: Viking Press, 1960), 359.

When loving you, Divine Mother,
my mind is focused easily on you.
All personality aspects stop
their clatter.
Great endurance is needed—
accepting Your challenges—
to be victorious.
What has ordinary life to offer?
In marriage
the mating dance is soon over.
In career the heart remains empty.
Art in various applications
bypasses the hunger.
The monkeys have eaten the bananas,
the mangoes are not ripe yet.
Who is it that dwells in me,
drying up the well of emotions?
Must I go elsewhere
to quench this great thirst?

3 *Sex*

As we have seen, for people in the first three stages of human development, sex is simply a biological function and a physical pleasure. For them, sex is gratification, and they approach it in the same greedy way they gobble food. The partners have little consideration for each other. Life for them is mostly a matter of survival. Such people are like leaves in the wind, blown hither and thither by life and destiny, and at the mercy of their own instincts, until they begin to think, and ask themselves, Does it have to be this way?

Although we can be on a lower level in regard to sex, we may be more developed in other ways, because no one is completely at one level. We could be highly developed in many areas, but without the understanding and discipline necessary to redirect or transcend the sex drive. There is within everyone a constant interplay of all the human forces: instincts, attitudes, and traditions.[1]

The instincts that in the past have served primitive human beings for survival in the world, still exist in today's marketplace. And in order to understand the modern over-valuation of physical sex, we can perhaps recognize it as an extension of that survival instinct. The purpose of sex is procreation, so that the human race will continue, just as it is for the continuation of any other species. But the world is now overpopulated, and there is little need for any race to worry about propagating the species. Today, human beings must regulate the number of offspring they produce before they find themselves forcibly regulated. It is time to recognize that the creative power behind the sex drive has another purpose.

Human beings have always tried to make of sex something more than its basic function of procreation. Even in primitive societies, those that do not yet have even a written language, sexual taboos exist. It is as if we have always known that there is more to being human than just procreation. Human beings are the only animals that have a consciousness of themselves and can think of themselves as "I am" or "I know that I am." Having this consciousness is a sign that they are moving out of the animal kingdom. If human beings had been born for no purpose other than physical and sexual satisfaction, humanity would never have risen to a state where the word *consciousness* could come into being. This evolution carries with it the responsibility for us to recognize and transcend the power of the instincts.

Sex is bound up with the human cycle of creation: birth, life, and death. Along with the gift of life inevitably is given the experience of human suffering—the pursuit of pleasure and avoidance of pain—and eventual death. In order to evolve beyond the limited perception of instinctual being, we need the courage and humility to seek an understanding of Divine Law, and to bring it into our lives through personal ideals and the power of choice.

To take responsibility for a sexual relationship means either to accept the possibility of pregnancy, or to use effective birth control methods. We have become clever enough to tamper with the stream of nature by devising methods of contraception in order to prevent the inevitable fear of pregnancy from interfering with our pleasure. But for anyone who is trying to evolve, there is the requirement not to allow the sex act to be merely the pursuit of pleasure. If we do not accept responsibility for birth, it means we do not accept death, since they are linked together as two parts of the same unit.

Today we try in many ways to deny death. Most of us turn away from people as they get old. Their approaching death reminds us that we, too, have to face it someday, so we look the other way. If we cannot accept birth as a consequence of sex, we do not accept death as a consequence of life. Nature has made the basic purpose of sex very clear, and we must accept responsibility as much for the production of new life as for the fading of life that has existed.

When the male is at the level of instinctual functioning, he is a victim of the pressure of nature. In the Old Testament man is called "the seeder"[2] because of this pressure to engage in sex with woman in order to discharge the semen, or the seed, and impregnate her. Similarly, the female is tricked by nature into the continuation of life, and her need to create a home to nurture her offspring. It has therefore been necessary for the woman to try to be a sexual being to please the man. Men and women, both, are in the grip of blind instinct when they approach sex without discrimination.

This "mating dance," the same one we see throughout nature, is what we usually mistake for love.[3] We are familiar with the male animal's display that is designed to attract the female and to persuade her that he is a suitable mate. Often this takes the form of a fight between the suitors, sometimes to the death. Is this different from men's struggle to prove their superiority through competition for power and prestige, the daring feats or tests of skill that show their supremacy?

Perhaps one of the most spectacular of the mating dances is that of the peacock, spreading his tail and strutting to gain the attention of the peahen. We have reversed that, and today the woman is usually the more colorful and attention-getting. Women play many games designed to catch a man. The coquettish mannerisms that tell a man he is the most wonderful thing that ever happened can be seen in women of all ages—from six to sixty, or more.

In some relationships the mating dance lasts a little longer than in others, but because procreation is the primary purpose of the sexual act, after some time the attraction and the desire are gone. The man becomes attracted again and again to other women because that is the law of nature. Women do not follow that instinct quite so readily because they are more aware of its consequences, and because of the likelihood that they will become emotionally involved. When we are caught up in the mating dance it is impossible to see that the basic functions of seeding and nurturing have other purposes, beyond those of nature's, in the development of a fully human being.

In modern life there are more subtle traps to catch women. One of them is the man-made idea that claims a "healthy" sex life is necessary for our physical well-being. And yet we seldom recognize that the intense sexual urge does not come from the body. Through mind the interpreter, the pleasant sensation from a caress on the skin sets in motion all past experiences, and results in desire. That desire is in the mind, not in the body. When sexual gratification is involved, we seldom apply logic. Only people who have developed their power of discrimination have the awareness necessary to distinguish their fantasies from the facts.

Swami Sivananda[4] has said that every woman whom a man lures into his bed must in some lifetime become his lawful wife. In North American society a young man learns very early that one of his highest goals is to get as many girls into bed as he can. That attitude places him at the very lowest level of evolution as far as sex is concerned. But he can change it by cultivating gratitude for his mother, who nourished him with her own blood and body, gave him birth, and prepared him for life by training and protecting him. In yogic thinking, all of us have chosen our parents in order to complete another step in our evolution. If we acknowledge that we made that choice, it helps us to elevate sex from the level of self-gratification and pleasure into one of responsibility.

When we find ourselves attracted to someone of our own sex, we must assess if the basis of our attraction is "I want the pleasure, but not the consequences." However, in some instances the homosexual or bisexual person may have come into life, this time in the opposite sex, in order to fulfill a relationship that had not been completed in another lifetime. From the yogic point of view, a homosexual has not made a precise adjustment in the change of sex from the previous life, and so deserves no criticism or judgment.

Sex is not bad in itself, but it becomes so if it is used without discrimination and responsibility. The degrading language that Westerners use in connection with sex, the degrading way of thinking about sex and of making each other sex objects, is the result of misunderstanding its essential qualities, which in reality can lead to our enrichment and to fullness of life. But we have to look into our own temperament to see if we really live by the principles we have set up for ourselves. We must understand our body and its functions, as well as the laws of nature. The purposes of sex are procreation and creativity, not gratification and pleasure. If we do not accept that, we can expect difficulties of all sorts, because we cannot turn nature around and make it what it is not. But by respecting the laws of nature and living by our principles we will elevate sex from the level of instinct to one of responsibility.

Those of us who are attempting to become aware individuals, free from mass hypnosis and the control of others, must give careful thought to the moral, ethical, psychological, and spiritual implications of all the issues surrounding sex. It is important to see, as clearly as possible, what is taking place in the society in which we live, in order to maintain personal integrity and some freedom of choice.

The manipulation and control of human sexuality for monetary gain has become a dangerous power game in the hands of economic giants, and has extracted a high price in pain, suffering, disease, and abuse.

The sale of birth control products has become big business, reinforcing the pleasure principle in sex. Blatant as well as subconscious techniques in advertising and entertainment are used to manipulate our basic sexual drives. In fact, there is a relentless barrage of propaganda that pushes sex as the panacea for every problem.

People who are still sleepwalkers, with little awareness, fall victim to this manipulation. The result is often the unwanted child, who can become the target of child-beating, incest, emotional abuse, child labor, or child prostitution and pornography, to name just a few of the reported atrocities.

History has shown that in many primitive or even developed societies, the children of a rival tribe have been killed. The offspring of the enemy are not thought of as innocent children, but as potential enemies and tools of revenge. While the methods may have changed throughout history, their effects have not.

Many other ugly pictures of abuse have emerged from our history, particularly in connection with the weak, the aged, women, and children. It is a merry-go-round to which even the most compassionate, with the greatest reverence for life, have not found a solution. One is reminded, sadly, of the statement in the Old Testament that the sins of the fathers are visited on the children up to the third and fourth generation.[5]

Even as newborn babies, children are found battered or abandoned. Research in this area is heartbreaking and shows that throughout history, regardless of the culture or the country, life has had little or no value. Children have been used as cheap labor, and daughters as pawns for bringing wealth to the family. Until recently child labor was the norm for the lower classes. Today the powerful few, in the name of the buying and selling of companies, of trading and merging, cause suffering not only to children, but entire families, and destroy their ability to survive in the battlefield of economics.

With technology now able to do such things as discover the sex of the embryo during pregnancy, one wonders what we are heading for. The possibility that technologically-monitored pregnancies could become compulsory is a sobering thought, and is an example of elite medical and scientific power groups infringing on the rights of individuals.

The overpowering of the female by the male has been found in basic sexual attitudes the world over. Even today there are few males who will give affection without expecting sexual gratification. This is exploitation, taking advantage of a human need, and is a manifestation of tremendous selfishness. Most women cooperate in this exploitation to have their need for affection met. But when people use each other simply for gratification, the seeds of resentment have been sown.

The number of unwanted babies gives an insight into the fact that the female does not lovingly accept the offspring of a male who has left her. Perhaps for nature, with its extravagance of seed, that is a fact of no significance, but for the individual human life it is an important point. For a child, survival does not depend only on food and clothing, but also on emotional care and acceptance. We have to recognize that as human beings we have a responsibility to children beyond nature's pressure to procreate.

People also need to have a sense of worth about their bodies, and they need to be discriminating about whom they share the vibrations of their bodies with. Although sex is a much-discussed topic of conversation, we seldom recognize its power. Before engaging in sex both partners know who they are, but at the moment of climax they lose their identity. What perhaps neither observes is that this loss of consciousness, even for a very brief moment, has been preceded by an interchange of emotional and vibrational forces that may not benefit either of them. If a person frequently has interference from someone else's vibrations, he or she may lose a lot of what is his or her very own. Men need to be discriminating about the woman or women they choose, because of the emotional clinging of many women. Women need to choose carefully to avoid the violence or resentment present in many men.

It is for these reasons that, from the yogic point of view, sex is not seen as sin, but rather as a hindrance to spiritual development. And although modern life makes the satisfaction of sexual desire easier—because one can just walk out of the life of the other person—as our awareness increases, we realize that self-seeking actions do not fit well with seeking higher values in life, or with becoming a more compassionate being.

When we wish to become masters of our own destiny, we must recognize external conditioning and internal compulsions, and the choices that we need to make. Recognizing the power of choice allows the transformation to take place from the state of the "human animal"—content to eat, sleep, and procreate—to that of a fully "human being." Clarification is the first step in putting ideals into practice in all aspects of our life, including sexual relationships.

There is within each one of us a hidden potential that urges us to search for something higher, to expand awareness, to develop the highest possible consciousness. Following blind instincts is not fulfilling; instead, it creates greed and indulgence. When we are in the first stages of development we have little understanding of sex; but as we evolve, an increasing awareness may become evident by our seeking out a partner with similar goals. Gratification, pleasure, and exploitation give way to a dawning in mind and heart that sexual activity could become sexual love. It is an enormous struggle for us to break free from nature's insistence on the continuation of the human species, but those of us who are able to do so have freed ourselves from the compelling drive of the instincts.

The first sign that we are closing the door to animal instincts may be the hymen. Why does no animal except the human female have a hymen?

There have been many customs that show almost an obsession with the issue of defloration. In some countries, it is the wedding veil that is symbolic for the hymen; sometimes the bride's veil is knotted to a loose scarf worn by the bridegroom. In some cultures the priest takes care of the defloration, with relatives of both families as witnesses. In medieval Europe the king might have a short-term encounter with a young female who was to his liking, then demand that one of his unmarried retinue marry her.

In all of these practices, the breaking of the hymen is a symbol of the power of the man over the woman. In the yogic concepts of the East, the hymen—left undisturbed, unbroken—symbolizes something quite different. The hymen is symbolized by the drum used by the devi, or goddess. This drum is a small device that is shaped like an hourglass, with skin covering each end, and with a string tied around the middle. To the string is attached a seed that will hit either end of the drum, but will never penetrate the skin.

By avoiding penetration, the use of the drum promises a two-fold experience (in contrast to sexual bliss): the attainment of knowledge, and the fruit—Higher Consciousness—that emerges from the dark womb of the mind. Because it is the devi who holds the drum, it is the female who destroys illusion. The movement of the seed on the end of the cord indicates the method: the practice of constant repetition, and hearing the chosen sound; or as we would say, "drumming it in."

The questions that arise from the symbolism of this drum are: Do I want to penetrate or be penetrated for human procreation, sexual pleasure, and the continuation of the family? Or (as in the case of extraordinary individuals like Ramakrishna[6]): Shall I penetrate the womb of divine wisdom? This is a serious choice that each of us can make. It must be clear that whether the seed will be the creator of new human life, or divine wisdom, it needs to be nourished to full maturity.

When we are moving toward the recognition of a Higher Self, we cannot maintain the views held by Mineral-, Vegetable-, or Animal-Man about sex and life. As we cultivate ourselves, we also change our ideas about sex. Human sight has been extended with the use of the telescope, hearing with radar, and perhaps we will now understand that we can also extend our experience of sex beyond its physical limitations. By understanding that physical union symbolizes the spiritual union of individual consciousness with Cosmic Consciousness, we can elevate sex into the world of the spirit, of consciousness. But here, as everywhere, it is the exceptional individual who has the courage to be different.

The sexual self is in contrast to the spiritual self. Between the pleasure-seeking sexual self and the Higher Self there is a tremendous range of awareness. It is our individual choice which one we select. Every one of us exercises the power of choice, although we often do not recognize that fact. We think we are driven this way or that, but in reality we are responsible for the decisions we make.

In the fourth stage of human development, becoming truly human means that we must strip ourselves of all excesses, the constant indulgence of self in every area.[7] Because each one of us has belonged at one time to the lower levels of evolution, we should be grateful that, by cooperating with our own evolution, we have been able to move into the next level.

The yogis of India make the point that in a hundred thousand lifetimes we have already experienced sexual bliss and the fulfillment of desires, and still we have not attained complete liberation. We may exhaust the energy that is available to us unless we begin to understand what we do, and recognize that we need to change our goal.

It must be remembered that every one of us has been created for another world—the spiritual world—as well as this one, and each of us is the bridge between these two. We all have a material physical body, and an intangible elusive mind that creates its own worlds and can take us to unimagined heights of the spirit. Those who wish to walk across the bridge must be willing to make the effort, and pay the human price for the bliss of spiritual union.

NOTES

[1]For anyone interested in further exploring this interplay, see Margaret Adams, "The Delicate Toils of Sex," and, "The Dumb Beast's Real Role," in *Single Blessedness: Observations on the Single Status in Married Society* (New York: Basic Books, Inc., 1976).

[2]Genesis 13:15-16. The Lord speaks to Abraham: "For all the land which thou seest, to thee will I give it, and to thy seed for ever. I will make thy seed as the dust of the earth: so that if a man can number the dust of the earth, then shall thy seed also be numbered."

Psalms 112:2: "His seed shall be mighty upon earth: the generation of the upright shall be blessed."

[3]Andrea Sachs, "Secrets of the Mating Game," *Time* (May 1, 1989): 74. Report on a study done by psychology professor David Buss of the University of Michigan. The study appeared in the psychology journal, *Behavioral and Brain Sciences,* and involved people in thirty-three countries to determine the relative importance of thirty-one traits in a marital partner.

"The reason for such universality . . . is reproduction: 'These are adaptations to the problems that males and females have to solve to reproduce and survive.' A woman will usually look for a prosperous man because he is better able to support a family, whereas a man will look for a woman whose age and appearance signal fertility."

[4]Swami Sivananda Saraswati of Rishikesh, India, was my Guru. Refer to *Radha: Diary of a Woman's Search* (Porthill, ID: Timeless Books, 1981) for the story of my time in India with Swami Sivananda.

[5]Exodus 20:5: "Thou shalt not bow down to them nor serve them: For I the Lord your God am a jealous God, visiting the iniquity of the fathers upon the children unto the third and fourth generation of them that hate me;"

[6]An account of Ramakrishna's experience in the practice of Tantra Yoga is given in Part II, Chapter XI of Swami Saradananda's *Sri Ramakrishna: The Great*

Master (Mylapore, India: Sri Ramakrishna Math, 1952).

[7]Mircea Eliade, *Yoga: Immortality and Freedom* (New York: Pantheon Books, Inc., 1958), 49–50. "The restraints *(yama)* purify from certain sins that all systems of morality disapprove but that social life tolerates. Now, the moral law can no longer be infringed here—as it is in secular life—without immediate danger to the seeker for deliverance. In Yoga, every sin produces its consequences immediately. . . . These restraints can be recognized by all systems of ethics and realized by an apprentice yogin as well as by any pure and upright man. Their practice does not result in a specifically yogic state, but in a 'purified' human state, higher than that of common humanity."

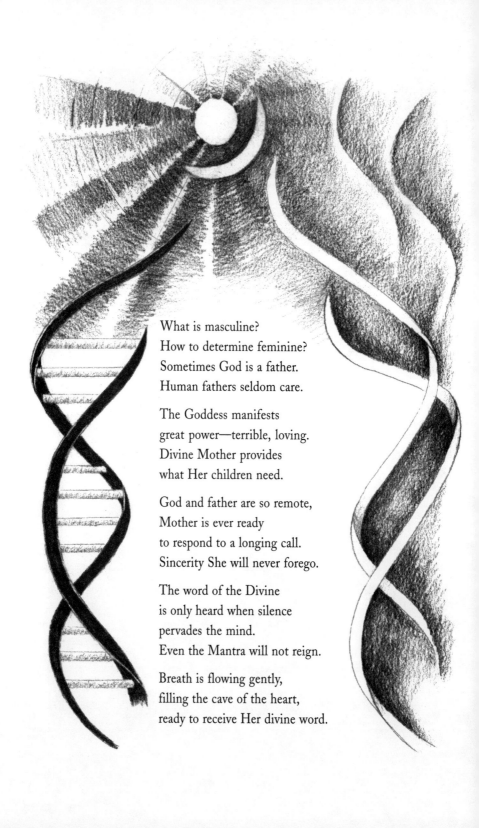

What is masculine?
How to determine feminine?
Sometimes God is a father.
Human fathers seldom care.

The Goddess manifests
great power—terrible, loving.
Divine Mother provides
what Her children need.

God and father are so remote,
Mother is ever ready
to respond to a longing call.
Sincerity She will never forego.

The word of the Divine
is only heard when silence
pervades the mind.
Even the Mantra will not reign.

Breath is flowing gently,
filling the cave of the heart,
ready to receive Her divine word.

4 Man and Woman

THROUGHOUT HISTORY the biological differences between men and women have dictated the way in which the sexes have regarded each other, and this has been reflected in their social and psychological attitudes. Physically, man and woman need each other, and the force that draws them together is nature's strongest instinct.

A well-known story in India points clearly to the difficulties that sexual passion poses even for the gods. One handsome young god had no difficulty in seducing women, even the wives of other gods, who complained bitterly about such behavior to Divine Mother. She scolded him severely, but to no avail. She mused on how this situation could be solved, because she herself is incarnated in each woman, and so the young god's actions were an insult to her. She decided to bring this to his attention. Every time the young god became inflamed with a beautiful female, Divine Mother revealed herself in the girl. The young god was startled; he could not make love to Divine Mother, his mother. He tried again and again, but the universe was filled with his mother's form and likeness. When he realized this, he became passionless.

This ancient story of Divine Mother and the young god is an indication that these problems are as old as humanity itself. The pain and agony as we emerge from the first three stages of development come from our struggle to enter the fourth level of truly human life. Even though we may realize the importance of moving away from instinctual urges, we lack the self-control and the willingness to take responsibility for the consequences of our actions. Until awareness is sufficiently expanded, we find ourselves over-reacting to being used, and then using others in return.

Men seem to be under more pressure from the power of nature, tempted to turn to women for sexual gratification, and then resenting their dependency. However, within every woman something remains of the inherited belief that she is only worth something if she finds a husband, and that she can discover herself only through a man.[1] With women outnumbering men in the Western world, many a woman is trying to do just that—find a man to discover herself! It will take a long time before this pattern moves out of the woman's subconscious and she realizes, "I am independent, I have a soul, I have a Higher Self, I do not need a man at my side to be complete, because I am complete."

Since the beginning of the feminist movement in the late sixties, an increasing number of women have explored what it means to be a woman, either in an intimate relationship or alone. These women are doing the pioneering work, offering other women the opportunity to understand their own uniqueness and develop respect for themselves as independent human beings. This work will provide a basis for a future psychology that includes both men *and* women.[2]

In the past there was no psychology of women because Western psychology was man-made. Man figured out and decreed what woman should feel, what she should think, and how she should behave. Otto Rank, in *Beyond Psychology*,[3] speaks of this in detail; he was the first psychologist to take women seriously enough to investigate their mental and emotional life.[4] In the story of the Tower of Babel, Rank says that although woman is reputed to chatter all day long, basically she says little, because she knows that nobody wants to hear what she has to say.

Women therefore live a secret life, having learned not to reveal their innermost thoughts and feelings. A woman can never be herself,[5] because man has created an image of her and has accepted that image so completely that he has put her out of his life. And what is the life of man? It is his profession, work, or hobbies, which he is often unwilling to permit a woman to enter.

Since the beginning of civilization, the male has tried to conquer the female and, having defeated her, has regarded her as his possession. Psychologists studying human development and sexual behavior, Wilhelm Reich in particular, have speculated that the act of male penetration can be seen as putting a knife into the woman, and that defloration, the breaking of the hymen, is an example of the conscious overpowering of the female by the male.[6]

Freud gave a paper in Vienna entitled "The Etiology of Hysteria" in April 1896, in which he presented his new theory that later became the seduction theory.[7] This theory accepted the validity of early childhood sexual abuse, and the detrimental effect it had on the lives of the victims, usually girls. Freud's subsequent decision, conscious or not, to give up his seduction theory may be at least partially responsible for his ridiculous statements about female penis envy.

The sacrifice of the scientist in himself by a man of Freud's stature was a sacrifice of women as well, and the resulting injury since then to women in general cannot even be measured. Rank, his disciple, had the courage to break away from Freud's ideas. He recognized that man has put woman entirely out of his life by refusing to accept her femininity. Rank also pointed out that early man's envy of woman caused him to try to dominate and subjugate her, and with few exceptions this has been the history of male-female relationships. Needing his protection while she gave birth and looked after her children, woman accepted his help, not realizing that it would lead to his domination over her.

Otto Rank speaks of man's "wastefulness." In the overproduction of semen (more than is needed for the creation of one baby), man is shown to be a mass-producer, which has now found its expression in the mass-production of goods. Even in the Old Testament man is called the "seeder," a testimony to the nature of the male, who is at the mercy of nature's biological urges. While woman is the nurturer, the tendency of man is to go outward, or, as the Buddha has stated, "Man ever wants to change the world."

Rank admits that in his research he has found that the female is not as interested in sex as the male. However, one who is subdued, who is enslaved, will do anything to please the one who is in control. Thus the woman plays at being sexually enticing. It is conceivable that there are many women who have developed the sexual urge, but did not have it in the beginning. While the female of the animal kingdom is protected by the seasons, the human female does not have the same protection. She may not use her consciousness properly because she fears that she must always say yes to her superior, the male.

Each woman must recognize in herself the barriers that she has put up for self-protection, and her desire to be accepted. Although she is no longer condemned for having "free sex," the male often makes her pay for the gratification of her need for love and affection by leaving her with the offspring. To be accepted, a woman sometimes goes to incredible extremes, almost to the point of self-destruction. Such a woman tries to live up to a man's expectations, and caters to him because she believes that is the only way he will stay with her. The prospect of having full responsibility for herself and her offspring is a frightening thought—almost like a whip to keep her subordinated.[8]

However, sex enslaves both men and women; once sugar is tasted it is wanted always. Clever women of all times have been able to take all of his possessions from a man by manipulating him, and by withholding sex. History is full of stories of men ruined by such women, who were perhaps taking revenge for all their other disappointments.

But the reverse is more often the case. In some countries there are sad examples of men asserting absolute power over women. For example, in ancient Europe young girls were often abandoned, sold into slavery or into prostitution. We may think that the medieval age is over, but even today some traditions permit the marriage of girls at the very tender age of eight or nine, when they are emotionally and physically still children. Sometimes several brothers share the new bride; the strain on a young girl who is forced to satisfy a number of men is hard to imagine. Child prostitution is common in many Third World countries. In India the woman's place is clearly shown by the ancient practice of suttee, in which the wife is burned alive on her husband's funeral pyre. Despite the abolition of suttee, every year some cases come to light that have been carried out in great secrecy.

This act is often presented as a demonstration of the wife's heroic love for her husband, but it is more accurate to say that her life would be so miserable that death by fire is preferable to her status as a widow.

How did women fall into this miserable state? Did they at one time have power? Did they misuse it? Was their misuse of power responsible for bringing them into the state of subservence that has been theirs in recent times?[9]

Women need to study the development of their position within family and community.[10] Without such a background it is futile to expect women to change quickly. The section in the beginning of my book, *Kundalini Yoga for the West*, entitled "Woman, the Handmaiden of Divine Mother," draws women's attention to the qualities they do possess, and encourages them to appreciate their persistence in making changes and bringing order out of chaos. "Unless she realizes her role in this world drama and is willing to assume this responsibility, woman cannot emerge from her 'second position' but, more important, she will miss the purpose of her own life."[11] In order to take on their proper role, women must cut themselves free from emotional bondage and be willing to take responsibility for their lives.

The human tendency to create gods of leaders has been especially detrimental to woman. In some countries, such as Japan, the emperor was the embodiment of divinity. In medieval Europe, kings ruled by "divine right." Most kingly families obtained power through warfare, then surrounded that power with a halo. These powerful men used women as pawns—dominating and using them as objects. It was their custom to give their daughters and other female relatives in marriage to secure land, increase their power, and conclude treaties with neighboring rulers.

If we look into our own culture, we see that until very recently women could not have their own bank accounts but needed the permission of the husband, the father, or any male authority. Even cases of such gravity as rape or child molestation are still handled with velvet gloves by the male judges. The stereotype of the superior male is very difficult to remove but, by the same token, the image of the helpless woman makes it difficult to believe that she could perform a vicious and cruel act, or even commit murder under the compulsion of emotions.

In some cultures, young men and women were trained equally for warfare, but the women were not sent into battle unless it was absolutely necessary because, while one man can have numerous offspring, a woman can generally produce only one child at a time. Because nature has given that particular pattern to men and women, the tendency for the average man will be to take any sexual opportunity that is offered to him.

On the other side, women fail to recognize that their need for affection is often stimulating to men, and is therefore misunderstood as a sexual invitation. Most women do not think about the purpose of nature (which is to recreate itself) or the power of the sex drive. Thus women try to overrule nature's design for men—propagation of the species. They also do not want to deal with the fact that their own desire for children is primarily nature's design, through the working of their biological clock. Both men and woman need to recognize these instincts at work and redirect their energy if they are to emerge from the Animal-Man level.

Also, Western woman has to recognize that she has become very aggressive in the mating dance, making herself a temptation to men, dressing in a provocative way. Enormous industries have been developed to give her the means of doing this—in North America there are annual sales worth billions of dollars in cosmetics alone—and these, interestingly, often have been created by powerful women. This provocation is very difficult to withstand for a man who is still primarily in the early stages of development—the instinctual man who lacks self-esteem—and is often part of the reason for disloyalty in marriage.

Women of today have to be particularly careful to clarify what they really want. In daily life the woman often wants to have the masculine man and the gentle understanding one at the same time. She longs for the cavalier, the protector, yet also demands to be an equal. The women's revolution has shown up these discrepancies very clearly; for many, that process of change is still going on. Indeed, the time of revolution has been too short for women to understand themselves. Women want to claim their rights, despite the fact that many have not yet achieved the freedom from compelling emotions that is necessary for them to make wise decisions. Most women also lack the maturity to handle any newly-won freedom wisely. Although today many women are economically independent, their emotional and sexual dependency still causes them problems. Women have to learn to look more closely at the facts in even the best of relationships.

A woman's struggle for survival is shown in her concern for what others think, her fear that she will be ostracized if she is alone. She has no way of existing in her own eyes if she is enslaved by her fear of others' judgment. The need for acceptance can be seen even in the successful professional woman. A woman usually can become successful in the business or professional world only by imitating men, because that is the only way in which men will accept her, making it very difficult for the career woman to maintain her femininity.

Today single women especially live in the danger and fear of being raped. Because of this fear, women who live alone tend to think that it would be better to have a husband. Women have had to regulate and limit their lives to protect themselves, so they will not be seen as objects of a temptation to rape that men will not control. Even now, when a woman is raped during some innocent activity such as jogging, or coming home from a movie theater, she is often accused of having provoked the attack. She is to blame. In many cases the pregnancy that results cannot even be terminated, and there is one more unwanted child whose life will be hell.

While we may think that these ideas are changing, the change is occurring in a very small percentage of the population. Deep in a man's subconscious, his wife is his property. A well-known scientist whose wife was also an acknowledged scientist could not accept the fact that his wife was recognized in her own field. Although she had all the credentials and background as a scientist, for him to accept her achievements would have diminished his importance as a man.

Similarly, a woman with a great talent in acting or music cannot become an outstanding performer without male support to climb to the top of the ladder of fame. Talent alone is seldom sufficient. Sexual powers, or the pretense of such powers, will open doors for her.

However, women have a responsibility to realize the power that they do have, to face themselves and see where they have manipulated others. Women must stand up for themselves and not allow themselves to be used, but they must also take care not to use men for their own convenience and comfort. They must grow beyond the idea of a Dream Lover, and their need to have some male to worship.

All of us have a Dream Lover tucked away in our minds, regardless of whether we are married or single. It can distort our perceptions of another, either positively or negatively, and it is a merciless taskmaster, a standard of perfection that can never be achieved. The woman may be looking for a man who is both commanding and sensitive. The man may want the Virgin Mother herself for his wife, but the prostitute for his pleasure. For her, the ideal of a Dream Lover may raise conflicting demands for security and equality. For him, the Dream Lover is at odds with his sexual instincts. To release ourselves from the grip of the Dream Lover, we must look within ourselves for that part that needs to mature and grow up. There is in every man a little boy, and in every woman a little girl. If we want to satisfy those little ones in ourselves, and if the attachment is so great that we cannot give up that satisfaction, we may as well forget the pursuit of spiritual life. The demands are too high, the requirements of strength and maturity too great. But if we can bring those little girl and little boy aspects to maturity, we can break the grip of our unrealistic expectations.

The place in each other's lives that will most benefit both men and women is that of friendship. What a man needs is a travel companion through the difficulties of life, not a woman who plays the helpless creature, or one who uses motherhood for self-gratification and recognition. A woman can be helped and encouraged by her partner to recognize that she possesses intelligence and logic, and the ability to apply both.

Women who do not want to look at facts (because facts are cruel), cling to their illusions, but illusions are only temporary, and one day they will be recognized for what they are: the cause of pain and bitterness. The discipline necessary to look at the facts is not natural to most women, so they will have to make the effort to develop it. Quality must be in all aspects of a woman's life, every day, in all actions, meeting her own standards, and facing herself clearly. Instead of scattering her energies through chatter, she should talk to that woman deep down inside and allow her to come forth. When Jesus said he would make women male so that they, too, could enter the Kingdom of Heaven,[12] he meant that they would develop the power of reasoning and logic. Equality for women means emotional independence and acting with reason.

I have met *brahmacharis* (celibates) in India who said that they were praying to be reborn a woman because women have inborn devotion. That inborn devotion is a beginning. Women, through their femaleness and intuition, have been imbued with an inner knowledge of the mystery of life that men lack and try to recreate in many ways. Men on the spiritual path can begin to develop their own feminine qualities of receptivity, nurturing, and creativity through reflection and self-investigation—basic tools of Yoga. And women can acknowledge and develop their own strength of intellect, reason, and ability to act logically.[13]

All human experiences are meant to help us along the path of evolution and, if we accept the challenges, they will enable us to develop our consciousness.

NOTES

[1]M. Esther Harding, "All Things to All Men." Chapter 1 in *The Way of All Women: A Psychological Interpretation* (New York: G. P. Putnam's Sons for the C. G. Jung Foundation for Analytical Psychology, 1974).

[2]Margaret Adams, "Psychology's Distorting Prism 1 & 11," in *Single Blessedness: Observations on the Single Status in Married Society* (New York: Basic Books, Inc., 1976). Adams has written a generous and unapologetic celebration of unmarried life in a married society.

[3]"There actually are two different languages characteristic of man and woman respectively, and the woman's 'native tongue' has hitherto been unknown or at least unheard. In spite of her proverbial chattering, woman is tacit by nature; that is, she is inarticulate about her real self. Man, in his creative presumption, took

upon himself the task of voicing her psychology—of course, in terms of his masculine ideology. This fundamental misunderstanding between the two sexes, speaking as it were different languages, appears in Biblical tradition at the beginning of things when Adam listens to the voice of the serpent, speechless by nature, and simply understands it his way." Otto Rank, *Beyond Psychology* (New York: Dover Publications, 1958), 243.

⁴Writing four decades later, Carol Gilligan says, "The disparity between women's experience and the representation of human development, noted throughout the psychological literature, has generally been seen to signify a problem in women's development. Instead, the failure of women to fit existing models of human growth may point to a problem in the representation, a limitation in the conception of human condition, an omission of certain truths about life." Carol Gilligan, *In a Different Voice* (Cambridge, MA: Harvard University Press, 1982), 1–2.

⁵Carol Gilligan in interviewing women was once asked, "Would you like to know what I think or would you like to know what I *really* think?" See *Ideas,* "The World According to Women." Toronto: Canadian Broadcasting Corporation, 1991. Transcript of a radio series. Gilligan describes how girls disconnect from their real experience and substitute the dominant male voice of the culture, learning to distrust their own experience.

⁶Research conducted at New York Medical College on the sexual habits of politicians and top executives led the researcher to conclude that "for many politicians and executives the power drive and the sex drive become so closely linked that they become one and the same." Matthew Fox, *A Spirituality Named Compassion* (San Francisco: Harper & Row Publishers [1979] 1990), 65.

⁷Jeffrey M. Masson, "Freud and the Seduction Theory," *Atlantic Monthly* (February 1984),: 33–60. In his research, Masson found that Freud sacrificed the scientific evidence he had discovered about childhood sexual abuse in order to be more acceptable to a superior male scientist.

On page 36 of the same article, ". . . the abandonment of the seduction theory prepared for the birth of psychoanalysis."

And on page 60, "The analyst who sees a patient with memories of sexual abuse is trained to believe . . . that those memories are fantasies. An analyst trained this way, no matter how benevolent otherwise, does violence to the inner life of his patient and is in covert collusion with what made her ill in the first place."

⁸Jean Baker Miller observes, "A subordinate group has to concentrate on basic survival." Jean Baker Miller, *Toward a New Psychology of Women* (Boston: Beacon Press, 1976), 10. Chapter 1 describes the interplay of dominant and subordinate groups, particularly men and women.

⁹There is scant evidence of ancient matriarchal rulership, but some traces can be found. The Amazons are said to have created an efficient society without men.

[10]Gerder Lerner, *The Creation of Patriarchy* (New York: Oxford University Press, 1986). Lerner describes the relationship of women to history, explains the nature of female subordination, and the causes for women's cooperation in the process of their subordination.

[11]Swami Sivananda Radha, *Kundalini Yoga for the West* (Spokane, WA: Timeless Books, 1978), 31.

[12]"Jesus said: See, I shall lead her, so that I will make her male, that she too may become a living spirit, resembling you males. For every woman who makes herself male will enter the Kingdom of Heaven." A. Guillaumont, trans., *The Gospel According to Thomas: Coptic Text Established and Translated* (New York: Harper & Row, 1959), 57.

[13] For a description of the importance of reconciling the inner masuline and feminine principles in both men and women in order to bring about a resolution of the outer conflicts, see Esther Harding, *Woman's Mysteries: Ancient and Modern* (New York: Harper Colophon Books, Harper & Row, 1976), 37.

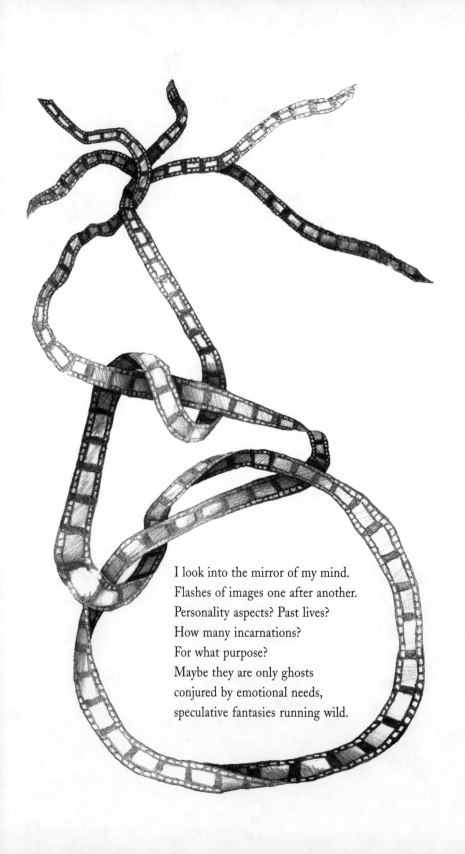

I look into the mirror of my mind.
Flashes of images one after another.
Personality aspects? Past lives?
How many incarnations?
For what purpose?
Maybe they are only ghosts
conjured by emotional needs,
speculative fantasies running wild.

5 *Why Marry?*

THOSE OF US who are approaching or who are already in the fourth level of development, that of Man-Man, will be seriously questioning the place of sex and marriage in our lives. Becoming truly human has a whole range of meanings, the most important of which is to take responsibility for one's life and evolution. And although the chemistry that works between two people on the physical, mental, and emotional levels cannot be eliminated, it must be understood that everything has its price. One does not become a virtuoso without a great deal of time, effort, and practice, and the same is true of becoming a truly human being.

When we are young we are not given sufficient education, nor are we wise enough, to realize what it means to enter into an intimate relationship, that there is a responsibility for working on that relationship and recognizing the possible results. We have a responsibility for offspring, and the very important questions of birth control and personal health. We must investigate very soberly what we want from a relationship, what our motivation is, and what we need on the physical level, whether or not sex is the driving force for entering into the relationship. We can prevent disappointment by being as clear as possible about these issues.

Disappointment is caused also by wanting what a partner is unable to give. We often must undergo much disappointment and heartbreak to realize that wanting somebody else to be responsible for our individual happiness is an impossible demand. We are each responsible for our own inner peace and happiness, and cannot expect it from anyone else; to expect that is like chasing an illusion.

We tumble into relationships, driven by social pressures, by instincts, by common habits, by biological urges, without any idea how many factors contribute to what we think is a truly personal decision. Looking for the satisfaction of our needs and the fulfillment of our illusions, having expectations and assumptions, and wanting the approval of another person are often the basis for feeling that our life is worth living and that we are indeed worthwhile. We must be clear about what we need, what we want, and how much we are willing to give up or even sacrifice in a relationship. Being clear at the beginning prevents one or both from later making hurtful accusations that may have little or no foundation.

There are no rules that apply to everyone. Each person will have to ponder these questions: Is sex just a biological function? Is sex only for procreation? What does the Kundalini Force have to do with sex? Should one practice celibacy? Is sex a creative force that can be channeled elsewhere? Is sex connected with psychic energy?

All questions of morals should come only from our own inner being, from our own convictions. Societal morals vary with the culture and the times, and what is expected in one part of the world is unacceptable in another. The taboos between the sexes are determined by the stage of human development within a society at a particular time. The institution of marriage came into human life to bring commitment into sexual relationships, and to control the interaction between men and women, based in part on the self-protection of the male who does not want to bring up the offspring of another male. However, as religious and spiritual ideas come in, changes take place. As we move along on the course of evolution, we begin to understand that the guiding principles come from a very different level: the union of the male and female within, of the rational and the intuitive, of the physical and the mental. And the purpose of spiritual life is eventually to lead us to that union between our Higher Self and our human self, which is the union all of us are really seeking.

We were not created to gratify appetites. We were created for another world also, and must bring together those two worlds—the human and the spiritual. To help understand that, stop for a moment and consider that you already know you are two beings: one is the physical body that is perceptible to our senses, and the other is the mental body that we cannot see or touch. Yet we are at all times in both worlds simultaneously, making it appear as if they were one. If we give this some thought we will realize that we always *are* living in two worlds.

Sex uses energy that can be colored any way the mind decides. The sexual act can be an unforgettable experience when both partners are able to overcome selfishness and are dedicated to cooperating with their own evolution. It is possible for two people to be married, or engaged in a sexual relationship, and also provide support for each other on the spiritual path. Those who can put the Divine first in their lives and their beloved second can have a happy relationship, yet at the same time live a spiritual life. However, to have the necessary control, both partners must first have achieved the spiritual marriage of the male and female within. This first spiritual marriage is the result of bringing into balance the rational and the irrational so that we can fully use the mind—logic and reason—in combination with the heart—feelings and intuition. It is this union that brings us fully into the fourth stage as a whole human being.

The moral standard of a sexual relationship is commitment. The morals are not dependent on having sexual relations or not, being married or not. Without commitment to the other person, there will be abuse, and that means the balance of the male and female cannot take place or has not yet taken place.

Mutual agreement, mutual love, and mutual commitment are necessary for a stable marriage. However, the first attraction when two people meet is usually physical attractiveness. When marriage is considered, the reasons range from wanting to get away from home, and being thought mature and important, to looking for companionship, pleasure, and security. There are even those whose egos are flattered if they are able to attract someone away from the spiritual path. Any who make themselves such a temptation create their own very bad karma.

There are beliefs and ideals deep within our consciousness that we have inherited from the culture to which we belong. But questions of loyalty, relationships, sex outside marriage, and monogamy must be answered by each one of us. The criticism and judgment we have for others must also govern our own actions. We cannot live by a double standard. The double standard is sin. Feelings of guilt and sin will be with us if we act against our ideals, and they will surface in moments of stillness. We must live what we believe in, and therefore we must clarify our own ideals and convictions, and we must put them into practice. The Christian cannot take on the moral convictions of the Muslim, or those of any other culture, without first doing this kind of clarification.

Two people who choose to be together in a sexual relationship outside marriage must both be willing to take responsibility for the consequences—the possibility of pregnancy. Individuals on the spiritual path will have to clarify their motivation for such a relationship. They must bring in common sense and discrimination to moderate their biological urges. There is within everyone the unconscious desire for union that creates those moods. We seldom understand that such a desire is really for a different kind of union—of the male and female within ourselves.

Those of us who feel that marriage is for us and that we would rather go through life married than not, must also clarify our reasons. It is unfair to marry in order to have an object of gratification for our emotional needs. Before marriage it is wise to be clear what kind of person we want to be, what ideals we hold of a husband, a wife, a father, or a mother, and what we would expect of our partner. When this is done there is less chance that either will have unrealistic expectations of the other. If the two people involved can be friends before getting married, the marriage has a good chance of surviving, and sex can enhance the relationship. It is therefore important to think of the characteristics and qualities we expect to find in a friend, and then turn within and ask if we have those attributes ourselves. Friendship is important in any relationship.

The ability to forgive is also an essential ingredient in any relationship, including marriage, so it is wise to investigate that quality, too, before taking this serious step.

It is very important to understand that the attraction is different for each of the sexes. A man perceives primarily through his eyes, and often chooses his wife or partner by the way she looks. A woman is generally attracted to a man by what he tells her. To marry on the basis of either kind of attraction is not enough. It is unfair to make demands afterwards, so by first becoming friends and establishing good communication, the couple can discuss their basic ideas and ideals before they marry.

People cultivate their five senses differently, so it is helpful for the partners in a relationship to find out which sense is dominant in each. Some men do not wish to have sex frequently, but like to touch their partner. If the most cultivated sense of the woman is hearing, it will be important for her that he talk to her. In this way, both partners can find out what their needs are, and by discussing them honestly can establish if they are willing or able to fulfill those of the other.

Many of us who think that we marry for the sake of love, do not know how we define the word *love*.[1] Often we are only in love with the idea of love, and of course that can also apply to being in love with the idea of marriage, fatherhood, or motherhood. We may be just experiencing a certain attraction that we need to define, or perhaps only attachment that is actually possessiveness. These distinctions are not easy to make, and love is difficult to define. The highest form of love has no "because" attached to it. When we use "because" to demonstrate our love for somebody, we need to investigate the reasons. They may have little to do with love; they may belong to the needs and gratification of some very human personality aspects. Until we reach the point where we can love with no "because," we cannot really know love.

Personality aspects[2] will always be with us. Each personality aspect can be compared to an instrument in a symphony orchestra. But rather than allow them to play out their parts forcefully and compulsively, the wisest decision would be to give the inner Self, willingly and with understanding, the position and power of conductor.

The senses, by which we experience and perceive life, lead to the chain of cause and effect through our desires and our efforts to gratify them. To make marriage into a relationship of support for mutual development, both partners must think deeply, try to gain understanding of the senses and their effects, and clarify their motives, ideals, and convictions.

Finally, we may realize that the only love is the love of the Most High, the Divine.[3] Perhaps that is the only love that truly exists, and as human beings with many frailties we cannot expect to give or receive perfect love. But it is wise to remember that even a love that is approaching the purity of Divine Love must express itself, otherwise it is worth little. It is through loving that the power of love increases.

Another thing to be considered is the influence that karma has on marriage. Many times a marriage takes place, not only through the choice of the individuals, but because it was necessary for these two people to come together again to bring a relationship into full flower. There are certain laws, extensions of the laws of nature, that can be called Divine Laws, and they must be fulfilled. In order to understand them, one must know what they are. They can be sought out in the same way that the laws of nature (such as electricity) are studied. If two people have not come together because of karma but by some other law of attraction, karma will be created in the present relationship that may force them to be reborn together at some other time. For that reason it is important to be careful either in getting married or divorced.

There is a saying that two human beings may each be half of the same whole, and this might be the basis of sexual magnetism. Perhaps we are in constant search of that other part of the soul of origination, and only because emotions and greediness interfere do we settle for less. If there is a possibility that there is another half, why should anyone settle for less? If people who want to marry would pray for their other half, perhaps fewer mistakes would be made. It is also possible that the other half is not on this earth, but guides the steps of the one who is here. It is worth pondering, looking into dreams, and keeping the possibility open of tuning in to that source of guidance.

In the story of the young gods from mid-heaven,[4] they projected love and beauty from themselves when they could no longer return to their Heavenly Home. Those who were most passionate became women, and these gods and goddesses then fulfilled their desires in one another. They imitated the animal kingdom to ensure the continuation of their existence, in the hope that in some future lifetime they would make it back again.

For those who wish to move out of the animal kingdom, the question arises of how to control sexual impulses and refine sexual relationships. The question should be asked with a feeling of intense homesickness for that Heavenly Home that was left, not from the needs of the self-asserting ego. To make our way back to our true abode we have to accept the possibility that we can free ourselves from traditional ways of thinking, and try to develop our higher natures.

Sexual energy is linked with the Kundalini Force, and it is part of the pranic flow in the body. It is important to adhere to the laws that will conserve this latent energy. If sexual energy or creative forces are scattered, it is like coming into life as a millionaire, wasting the money, and dying poor. Some yogis claim that we have only so many breaths, and our death is timed according to how fast we live our life. It is not a question of morals, but of conserving creative energy and channeling it into something truly creative.

We have a choice of continuing to engage in sex and using the sexual relationship as a means to reach the Divine, or attempting to transcend sex and using this Creative Force to build our own "Cathedral of Consciousness." For the practicing yogi it is a matter of choice and not of morals. This choice should not be made from the ego, which likes to consider itself different from most other people, thinking, "I am far along the Path, I can leave sex behind." This is the wrong motivation.

If we desire to reach the Divine but feel too weak to give up sex entirely yet, we should think, "Yes, I want to aim for the highest, but I am young and the temptations are great. Therefore I will take one step at a time." Or, if we find ourselves married, we might move toward the Divine by thinking that we will perfect our marital relationship. Thus we might say, "I will continue to have sexual intercourse, but when I do I will give love, rather than seek gratification for myself. Instead of having repeated sexual experiences, I will add more beauty and meaning to the act. Rather than making the sexual act one of self-gratification, I will have greater joy in the giving instead of the receiving."

The couple on the spiritual path who want to improve the quality of their sexual relationship will find that meditating together, or doing some other spiritual practice for half an hour before going to bed, will be most beneficial.

The ideal marriage is one in which the two partners consider themselves each one-half, together making a whole unit. In such a case, the man is then able to accept what is usually termed the irrational in the woman, and the woman will not be overawed by the rationality of the man. There will be an exchange, and each will bring out the best in the other. Where the idea of "I and Thou" exists, there is mutual respect, and there is no question of wanting only pleasure without the consequences or responsibility.

If it is possible for a person to preserve all sexual energy through the practice of celibacy, then there will be more to use for creativity. But if in practicing celibacy we use more energy fighting the sex drive than if it were indulged in, no energy is saved. Again, it is the ego wanting to be a celibate, or *brahmachari,* when we are not ready for it. Each of us must inquire within and pursue the path that is right. There is no prescription in life for everybody. Our own consciousness will make the best decision. The point is never reached where we can consider ourselves better or higher than others. If the struggle is less for some of us, a basic control in the area of sex may have been brought into this life.

As long as consciousness is embodied in the physical vehicle of the body, this vehicle is subject to the law of nature. However high our aspirations are, we must never condemn ourselves nor feel guilty when we fall below them. Everyone has the right to be a spiritual baby, and a baby is not punished when it cannot yet walk. Do not let the ego interfere and want to be a saint when you can barely crawl.

NOTES

[1]Alan W. Watts examines love in some detail in his chapter, "Sacred and Profane Love," in *Nature, Man and Woman* (New York: Vintage Books, 1970).

[2]"Everyone has many different personalities which move like actors into the foreground in various situations. The multitude of personality aspects is, in yogic symbolism, the covering dust of the glorious Self. In Western psychology it is often referred to as 'role playing.' The idea is basically the same." *Kundalini Yoga for the West,* 107.

[3]Erich Fromm provides thought-provoking material on the nature and elevation of love, in two chapters: "Is Love an Art?" and "The Practice of Love," in *The Art of Loving* (New York: Harper & Brothers Publishers, 1956).

Hari Prasad Shastri, trans., *Narada Sutras: The Philosophy of Love* (London: Shanti Sadan, 1963). The sage Narada explains the nature of devotion in a series of aphorisms *(sutras)* that, although of great antiquity, are still applicable to modern life.

[4]Jean Doresse, *The Secret Books of the Egyptian Gnostics* (New York: Viking Press, 1960), 316.

Lovers have their dreams and expectations.
They hope for eternal spring.
They see happiness everywhere.
They hear music that sounds sweet to the heart.
The imagination paints pictures,
         kindling expectations in ever-brighter colors.
This dream belongs to the world of the rainbow,
         in the far distance.
Illusory, no solid road leads to it.
The Royal Highway to life is cemented with reality
         that is often painful to walk upon.

6 *Marriage*

WE MUST WORK on relationships in all areas of life so that we can bring quality into them. Marriage is no exception. Both partners must recognize the many values in life—more than just the physical—that can be shared in a marriage relationship. There can be a meeting in awe at some marvel of nature or of human creativity, such as great works of art or inspirational music. There can be a meeting of minds in which ideas and insights flow back and forth between the two, producing greater inspiration for both. This is the kind of experience that creates a much stronger bond than leaving the attraction and interaction primarily at the physical level. For a marriage to grow and endure, reality must balance romanticism, quality must come into all aspects of life, with love becoming meaningful in sex, and the relationship flowering into one in which both sex and love have become significant.

The question is often asked if a couple can pursue spiritual life *together*. It is very difficult to find a partner equally interested in spiritual life. But even if both partners do have the same interest, what is meant by *together* needs to be clarified. It is an illusion to think that each person will progress at exactly the same rate as the other, or that together they will do the same practices, at the same times. They may not be attracted to the same path, and they may have different waking hours, different times when they feel inclined to do their practices. They may find that there is little they can actually do together.

As well, a woman's approach to life is not the same as a man's.[1] Her training and upbringing has been quite different, and that will have an effect on her spiritual life. She may be able to use her feelings and emotions to develop devotion in her spiritual practices through Bhakti Yoga. But if the man is caught up in rationality and logic, and has never learned to express emotions or feelings, he will have to take a different path, perhaps Raja or Jnana Yoga.

The path for both partners will constantly change. As they conquer one thing, they will go on to another. There can be no insistence that one partner do the same thing as the other, and they must accept the changes that take place. Patience, understanding, and willingness to wait, to accept whatever time it takes for both to do what they must, control of will and desire—these are what make a marriage spiritual.

It is important for any couple entering spiritual life to realize that each one is an individual, with an individual consciousness. Each has been born alone and will die alone. And everyone's development will be uniquely his or her own. But each can support the other on the way to their spiritual goal, and be truly together when they have reached that goal.

Our sexual activity changes as we change our views on life. In order to bring into focus the change in attitude toward sex, couples need to communicate, discussing it as openly as they would any other important topic. Otherwise sex is just "sex mechanics," remaining at the biological level.

If a couple clarify their expectations of each other, they can prevent the destructive guessing game in a marriage in which it is impossible always to guess right. Writing down a list of expectations of each other, then exchanging them and re-reading them occasionally, will help a couple to be aware how the relationship is developing. Pondering the events of their life together, whether promises have been fulfilled, or expectations lived up to, will keep the marriage alive and vital. Two people who are involved in a relationship of such closeness and intensity must try to help each other. Reflecting deeply each day, putting into practice what they know, and thinking before speaking will be mirrored in the quality of any couple's life.

Many young adults are woefully ill-prepared for life, and lack any realistic understanding of what is involved in a sexual relationship or marriage contract.[2] Too often a young woman is taught merely how to dress and make herself attractive to men. Education may help her catch a more suitable husband, but that is no guarantee that she will find a man who will stay with her for the rest of her life. If he has some ethical standards he might remain until the children have grown, but that does not necessarily happen. So without equality in employment opportunities and salary, she finds herself in a difficult situation.

Increasing numbers of women also are choosing to walk out on their husbands and children. It is difficult to imagine what is going on in the mind and heart of a woman who feels compelled to act so contrary to the ideal of the loving mother. Even if they are materially comfortable, however, many women are unable to tolerate a marriage that does not provide emotional satisfaction, open communication, or intellectual stimulation, despite the love they profess for their children.

Husbands and wives must talk to each other about dependence and interdependence, in order to reach an understanding of the difference. In dependency, any change becomes a threat. Interdependency exists for everyone—"no man is an island"—but we have to discover the purpose and goals of our individual lives. Each of us has a variety of goals—on the physical, mental, emotional, and spiritual levels. But they must be balanced so that one does not outweigh the others, and discussed so that the couple can maintain a common direction.

That balance will prevent sex from being overemphasized, so that it is not a primary motivation for being married. When the pleasure of sex is the driving force in life, we have little sense of responsibility for our offspring. If we decide to limit the number of children, or not to have any, the burden of birth control must be shared equally and not be put on only one partner, for that creates discrepancies that can throw an otherwise harmonious relationship out of balance.

A man's relationship with his wife and children is often his security; he feels they need him for their existence. However, after a time his interest in marriage or a close relationship may shift, because a man needs strong challenges that neither a wife nor a lover can provide.

Remnants of a distant past might linger on from a time when the fighting instincts were necessary to face the dangers of life in a hunting and gathering society. Those instincts are still present today, but not the challenges. And so there are always some men who seek danger in such sports as auto racing, aerobatics, or skydiving. For them, marriage and the peaceful life in a family is not enough of a challenge. Success in career, profession, or business is now what most men really aim for, although they say their family is the reason for their endeavors.

It is therefore not possible, or wise, for any wife to demand that her husband be responsible for her happiness. That is, in any case, a responsibility that no one can take for another person. It is the woman's choice what she wants to make of her life. Even if she is at home with small children, she can still nourish her mind and further her intelligence in many ways. Each of us must think first of putting quality into life, without making demands that our partner do the same thing. In their need for approval, there are still too many wives who want their husbands to participate in everything they do, apparently unable to do anything on their own.

The six stages of human evolution make it clear that a man and woman will make different decisions at different phases of their development. We must also remember that any plans we make and goals we set will depend on the family situation, and so it is wise to have several alternatives, which can be put into effect at various stages of family life.

Within the setting of the modern nuclear family, we must give consideration to the care of children if both husband and wife wish to work. For some it may be possible for each to work part of the year, although until women are given equal pay and opportunity, it is often financially unfeasible. However, such things must be discussed, so that later neither will feel resentful for being denied the chance to develop intellectually or through a career.

When there are children, it is the duty of both father and mother to talk to them as they grow up. A girl who wants to get married needs to be clear where she stands and what it means to combine a career and family. A daughter should also be assured that there is no shame in not being married. Unfortunately there are still women who marry because they feel it is expected of them.

A young man who wishes to marry must be helped to realize the responsibility and years of commitment he takes on to any children that he fathers. Parents must teach their sons, during their formative years, to look for a woman of good character to be the mother of their children, and not to get involved with women they are not willing to marry. A marriage seldom works if a woman becomes pregnant and has to marry because of the child. A woman wants to be married for her own sake.

The modern man who seeks sex for pleasure is the one who is most critical of the woman who has sex before marriage. Since sexual taboos are man-made, a means of protecting himself and his wife—his property in marriage—they are therefore a way of limiting his responsibility for children to those he fathers only with his wife.

Ideals and ethics impressed on the minds of young men will give them a sense of self-worth, and will be a guide throughout life, helping them to overcome the strength of their sexual drives.

Because woman has been destined by nature primarily for procreation, she has been given many characteristics to help her fulfill that function, including her irrationality: her mother instinct and her intuition. By not accepting them, man diminished her when he took over rulership. Woman still suffers from that image of inferiority, and so she still cannot live out her real feminine nature, which goes far beyond procreation.

When a couple avoid the primary function of sex—birth—it means they also avoid death, since birth and death are interlinked, and that leads to playing many deadly games. To find out what we really think about death, we can look first at some of these deadly games that are played in the marriage relationship. Seeking compensation through sex (which is similar to eating for emotional reasons) is a deadly game. We may use sex to punish or reward our spouse, or as a means of manipulation. All of this is an abuse of sex; it is a way to accomplish some other purpose. The one who thinks he or she must always be right is in a deadly game of competition. These games kill the finer feelings in a relationship.

We interpret many situations in terms of sex, because that is all we know. And often we do not know our reasons for choosing whether or not to take part in sexual activity. Indulging in self-pity, anger, fear, pleasure-seeking, boredom—these can be the stimulation for turning to sex. When we seek pleasure for ourselves in sex, we are incapable of giving. Pleasure-seeking leads to self-gratification, and the quality of a sexual relationship, and the marriage itself, will improve only when there is a giving of one to the other.

Many marriages may have come into being because of the emotional needs of either or both partners. Although emotional needs sometimes appear to be mental needs, they are needs of the ego: when we are concerned with fulfilling our needs, we are not interested in someone else's. Emotions are compulsive and must be brought under control. To do this we must have the ability to discriminate between what helps us and what is detrimental to us.

Pride is the antithesis of love. If we are too proud to say, "I'm sorry," we are incapable of loving. Love is little understood, and what goes by that name is more often compulsive emotions, swinging from one extreme to another. Perhaps love can be conceived of as being at the center, the steady point that allows us to keep the balance. We must, therefore, develop and nourish love through practicing care and concern for the other, and so develop beyond our need for our pride to be satisfied.

For the person with an authority complex, marriage is a fight for dominance, bound to fail. When we have this problem we must learn to look at facts and deal with our own egos, the real source of any authority issue. Only by honestly examining our motives and taking responsibility for all our actions and reactions, can we begin to understand that the culprit in any struggle for dominance is our own ego. There are two ways in which we learn: one is by loving obedience to the Divine Law, and the other is by being hit over the head by destiny. That is everyone's choice.

As long as we interpret situations in terms of sex, we will continue to undergo great suffering before we begin finally to think how we might improve the quality of our life, and what its purpose might be.

We must also look into some of the unpleasant aspects of sex. Until recently a surprising number of women have not known that there is much perversion in sex. Because sex has been turned into pleasure it has become a distorted force. In ancient times incest was a means of preserving the family clan, but such mistreatment continues today. It has become common knowledge how many children are being abused, not only outside the home, but within the family. For most people it is difficult to understand that fathers could abuse their own female children.

Whenever such abuse has taken place it has had a disastrous effect on the woman throughout her life, and on her marriage relationship. Few people have sufficient greatness of character for her to confide in them, without fearing that it would be later used against her. Such a woman carries this secret burden through all her life. Her instincts have warned her not even to tell her mother. In fact, many such incidents have been hidden deep in the unconscious of the woman herself, and it requires sensitive help to bring them to the surface where they can be dealt with. Fortunately, these incidents are now coming much more into the open. This allows other women also to have the courage to admit to themselves that they have been abused, and to look for the help they need.[3]

Ethics in love, sex, and marriage, as in any other human area, protect the innocent, the ignorant, or the weaker in any way from the abuse of power. Exploitation of another's emotional needs for self-gratification is not ethical, nor will it bring about a relationship of quality. Many of the ills from which marriages suffer are the result of such exploitation. Others come from feelings of guilt, which results from uncultivated imagination that magnifies previous failings. Infidelity causes injury to the partner's aesthetic sense, and generally results in the loss of compatibility. Even if forgiveness is genuine and there is no jealousy, it may be impossible to re-establish a sexual relationship. When aesthetics have been violated, the dynamic and expanding transformation that can come through sex, when it is engaged in with the right attitude, is frustrated and will not take place.[4]

The question of sexual intercourse outside marriage is one that all of us must answer from our own inner being. Whether it is injurious morally or spiritually must come from our convictions and ideals, not from the need for others' approval.

However, the creative forces within us should not find their expression only through sex. We must investigate, develop, perfect, and channel them. The full use of this energy in other ways will prevent greediness, feelings of merely tolerating or accommodating the needs of a partner in the physical relationship.

Couples who have been married for many years and become used to each other, taking each other for granted and becoming too attached, may reach a point where they want to make a new start. One or both may recognize the need for change, to improve and evolve. With cooperation and honesty, ideals and expectations can be discussed by the couple—as two human beings, as friends, as a wife or husband, as lovers. The habits that have kept the partners from closeness, and have brought insensitivity and numbness into their life together, can be talked over openly, with the approach of wanting to give a new look and new life to the marriage.

It is also important to investigate fully the Dream Lover image that all of us hold in our mind. This image of the perfect man or the perfect woman could be called a god or goddess, because such perfection is not possible on the human level. The man's desire to worship woman is in conflict with his conviction that he is superior. Whenever we put husband or wife on a pedestal, an unhealthy situation exists in the marriage, because the one we worship can never live up to our expectations. The only solution is for each of us to be independent within an interdependent relationship.[5]

Everyone, man or woman, has to find self-worth within, and that is where partners can help, by being supportive and bringing out the best in each other. To make a relationship more spiritual, the first step is to understand our partner and make no demands of the other that we cannot fulfill ourselves.

Married couples can make their sexual expression a special celebration. The mating dance that was a part of their life when they were dating can be brought into the marriage. We might think of this early intimate time as the prelude before the opera. And although constant togetherness does make people numb to each other, greater enchantment and romance can be brought into a marriage by as simple a step as having separate bedrooms. Individuality is precious, and everyone needs to be alone at times. This also allows us the freedom to live in a way that may be somewhat different from our spouse's way. Even two weeks of sleeping apart can bring a new attraction into the relationship.

Life, particularly married life, is made much more worthwhile by giving. We always receive in proportion to our ability to give. If we feel that for a long time nothing has been given to us, it means that we have not given and so are not eligible to receive. The sex drive is also God-given, and during the time of adjustment to a more spiritual way of life, while there is still sexual intercourse, it is important to consider that the pleasure we give to each other is of a divine nature if we make it so. The body is a spiritual tool that can be used to further the development of both partners. When we are more giving, there is more love than gratification.

Celibacy and sexual activity are obviously in contrast to each other, yet both are part of the same unit. Human sexuality, as we have seen, has been exploited. But we can take a new view to re-establish a true balance, so that our attitude toward sex can become a more wholesome part of our personal development. Periods of rest are necessary between times of creation in all of nature; maybe this applies to human beings also.

The yogic attitude to sex and celibacy is symbolized by the Hindu god and goddess, Shiva and Parvati,[6] and perhaps we can take them as an example for a new and different attitude.

Shiva dwells on Mount Kailas, a realm of ice and snow that symbolizes his asceticism. He sits there in continuous unbroken meditation. But he has also another aspect, for he is the god who danced creation into existence. He is often shown in a wheel of fire, representing passion. When Parvati, the goddess of creation, became Shiva's wife, the other gods of the heavens said, "What do you want with him, who has no place to offer you, who lives in ice and snow and takes the life of meditation?"

But when they came together and danced the beautiful Dance of Creation, the world came into being. Shiva represents unmanifest energy, and Parvati represents manifest energy. Both are necessary for creation to take place.

However, even the gods and goddesses need rest. Periodically Shiva returns to Mount Kailas, and Parvati, too, takes her times of celibacy. Asceticism and meditation allow time for renewal of energy before another period of creation. The same is true for us. We also need these times of rest, times that intensify our own personal magnetism. Couples who want a lasting relationship would be wise to think about this example of Shiva and Parvati.

Married couples can enhance their relationship by taking these periods of rest as a time to break habitual patterns, to renew strength and energy, to have the opportunity to delve deep within, come to an understanding of self, and continue the process of growth to wholeness, to all-round development. The yogic system provides many different paths suited to differing temperaments and stages of evolution, so each partner can choose what is best, and perhaps as a couple they may also find some practices they can do together.

The couple must be open in their communication, and frank about their aims. They cannot work toward celibacy unless both want it and are willing to improve their basic relationship first, showing love in ways other than by making physical demands. The nature of the entire relationship changes as the sexual relationship changes. Different ways are found of expressing love for each other, and finally each will see the other as a soul, as a companion on the road to Higher Consciousness.

But celibacy cannot be the aim of a married couple unless both have the same goal. It is unfair, if the marriage has come about under a completely different agreement, for one partner to try to impose celibacy on the other. If only one partner becomes interested in abstaining from sex, perhaps that desire can be taken as the opportunity to elevate the physical to a higher level, to become more giving, and in this way to spiritualize the relationship. The wife who is seeking Higher Consciousness can, by example, elevate her husband. And by the seeking of their parents, the children are uplifted. Husband and wife do not have to be on the same level of development, but they will need to have the same goal. With a common goal they will not hinder each other, and the one who is more advanced will simply have to practice patience.

For a man and woman to have a beautiful marriage she must accept his rationality, just as he must accept her irrationality. Bringing out the best in each other means also bringing out the best qualities of the opposite sex within oneself. The man must not suppress what is his birthright, intuition; the woman must learn to bring out her rationality where that is appropriate. The first mystical marriage—in yogic terms, the union of the male and female within—is sometimes announced by way of sex dreams. We cannot express oneness in any other way; when a man and woman attempt to become one in the act of sex, both momentarily lose their own identity.

Two people who are fully conscious of the responsibility they have to each other and to themselves, do not even need to make any promises to each other. They may sign a marriage contract because the culture demands it, but for themselves they do not need it.

There is something deep in the human mind that knows sex is not just for pleasure, and that the physical expression of sex really belongs only to a particular group of people who want to stay around the earth.[7] Those who seek a higher life of Cosmic Consciousness are willing to prepare for it by creating a good partnership and being friends in their marriage. This provides a good base in some other lifetime for a different kind of union, which is the meaning of the word *Yoga*. The purpose of each life is to bring us a step closer to that union of the individual consciousness with Cosmic Consciousness. In Chapter 11 there is a detailed exploration of the symbolism and the meaning of love in the story of Krishna, and in the Indian epic poem, the *Mahabharata*. This shows us the thinking that can lead our awareness out of our daily involvements toward a cosmic level.

Although for most people today the middle path is perhaps the best to choose (instead of celibacy), by bringing quality and mutual respect into our relationships we can make an act of worship of our sexual interactions. If we reflect upon the loss of identification that is experienced with the physical climax, our perception of the meaning of the devi's drum will expand. The pursuit of penetrating wisdom can then be a mutual undertaking between two people who have the same goal of Liberation, and who will grant each other the freedom that can be built only on trust. The degree of attachment and self-gratification is the deciding factor.

The realities of life and its daily demands, the emergence of challenges we must meet, give our mind the flexibility it needs to make the leap from the third into the fourth stage of development. Then subtle perceptions can be interpreted that, in the beginning, are difficult for the mind to understand. The wisdom of insecurity is one of the hardest lessons these challenges present.

NOTES

[1]Deborah Tannen provides a new approach to the battle between the sexes, showing the source of many difficulties in male-female relationships, which begin in the early stages of life. See "Different Words, Different Worlds." Chapter 1 in *You Just Don't Understand* (New York: William Morrow and Company, Inc., 1990), 43‒47.

See also, Gilligan, *In a Different Voice*. Gilligan contrasts the different approaches that men and women, boys and girls, take to issues of morality and relationship.

[2]M. Esther Harding, "Marriage." Chapter 5 in *The Way of All Women: A Psychological Interpretation* (New York: G. P. Putnam's Sons, for the C. G. Jung Foundation for Analytical Psychology, 1970).

[3]Boys, too, are subject to similar abuse, though the incidence is not so high as for girls.

[4]Alan W. Watts, "Consummation." Chapter 8 in *Nature, Man and Woman* (New York: A Mentor Book, The New American Library of World Literature, Inc., 1960), 156‒73.

[5]In cultures where young women are taught to worship their husbands, the men are expected to show the love and compassion that would make them worthy of such treatment.

[6]Wendy Doniger O'Flaherty presents an exhaustive study of sexuality in the mythology of Shiva and Parvati, showing both aspects: asceticism and eroticism. For those who are interested in expanding their understanding of the many levels of sex, her book is highly recommended. See *Asceticism and Eroticism in the Mythology of Siva* (London: Oxford University Press, 1973).

[7]Elisabeth Haich, "The Urge for Unity and Its Corruptions." Chapter 10 in *Sexual Energy and Yoga* (New York: Avon Books, 1978), 97–108.

The biological clock
ticks on and on,
no vision of future,
emotions flowing up and down
in an endless wave.

Beautiful fantasy
of a lovely child in my arms,
"corrupted by original sin."
Echoes of St. Augustine's voice.

How can there be love,
hope, and joy with the burden
of the past well into the future?
Dear Lord, is my child
not Your gift?
I asked for love.
You would not give me hate
Fill my heart with Your
wisdom. Guide my steps
so the child will live
for Your glory.

7 *Pregnancy and Children*

A LOVING COUPLE's joyful anticipation provides the positive attitude that has a profound effect on the baby during pregnancy and at its birth. During the time of pregnancy the surrounding influences have a great impact on both mother and child. If she is treated like a "queen of heaven," the bearer of a spiritual gift, her happiness will attract a highly developed soul in accordance with the principle that like attracts like. The Divine has very little chance to bring spiritual souls onto this earth, even though there are millions who engage in sex. Many souls have to choose selfish channels, which makes their life difficult. If the father is also involved in a natural birth process, the child will have a good start in this life, giving it the opportunity to fulfill its purpose within the Divine Plan.

In a couple's sexual interaction, when neither seeks gratification at the cost of the other, the flow of energy is not only from the sexual organs, but also from the heart and mind. For the couple who hold the attitude that in having a baby they open themselves to become channels for a new soul, their sexual expression may be repeated without harm during the time between conception and knowing that conception has taken place, which is about a month.

However, from the moment the woman knows that she has conceived, the baby should be allowed to grow undisturbed. This attitude is very important, rather than choosing to think, "Now that I am pregnant, let's have all the fun we can because I can't get pregnant twice." With such an attitude, the lower experience of lust interferes with the image of the child as a spiritual gift. Sex is not for gratification.

The partners in a good marriage who are trying to bring more quality into their lives have perhaps renounced sex in a previous life, learned a certain amount of discipline, and given the mind a direction, so that in this life sex could be given its proper place. Swami Sivananda said that parents who have no spiritual gifts to give are better not to have children. They will attract those consciousnesses or entities who seek to continue gratification, and who quickly acquire a new body so that they can continue what they were doing before.

To give a spiritual gift means that the parents look forward to receiving this little soul, and will do the best for it they are able, without either the father or mother thinking in terms of sacrifice. They will, of course, also regard the child as a spiritual gift to themselves. Such parents will work on their weaknesses, build character, and try to tune in with the Divine Forces. The emphasis in their sexual expression will be on the flow of love that forms a stream of Light. And that Light can be the channel for the new soul, one that is highly developed. Children should be invited, hoped for, prayed for, meditated about. They should not be accepted only as an unavoidable by-product of their parents' pleasure. They should be wanted for their own sake.[1]

The child who comes into this life unwanted has a very tragic life ahead. However, at one time there may have been a karmic condition in which good parents were not appreciated, so in this life conditions are reversed, and now the child feels rejected or simply tolerated. It could also be that in a past life there was great attachment to the father and mother, so in this one there are parents who do not care, in order to help the individual break attachment to family. If we attach our emotions to someone and become possessive, in another life we may be given a chance to undo that; in this way we learn balance, loving without wanting to possess.

Parents who have been willing to work on themselves, in order to become channels for a soul to come into life, are in a limited way conceiving through the power of mind, or spirit, over matter. And once the child is born, they must ensure that their ideals govern their actions. Then they will have no need to indoctrinate the child with religious lessons, because example is the best teacher. It is important that respect is shown for each individual in the family.

In terms of giving the child a proper sex education, parents should expect that children will be sexually motivated in their early years, simply out of playful curiosity. Sex should not be hidden, nor should children be taught to be ashamed of it. In the past in India, families kept their children close, giving them the skin contact at an early age that provides security later in life. The result of this seemed to be fewer problems with sex when the children grew up, because they had learned to accept their bodies naturally. The hidden sex games that adults play would be less popular if as children we had been taught a more natural approach to sex.

The consequence of premarital sex or sex outside of marriage is the possibility of illegitimate children, who are still not completely accepted in certain societies. The status of these infants must be legalized, and care be taken that they are given proper rights. Many of them are given up for adoption and, when they are grown, often feel that their dignity has been tampered with by having been denied even one natural parent. Living with the thought that one is the result of a sexual accident, and therefore not acceptable, is injurious to self-esteem. If sex can be seen as the means through which God creates children, who are his gift, destined to be born and to live, then all children must be given the care they need. When the government in power does not hold this conviction, then much more responsibility must be taken for individual sexual expression.

The society that encourages and promotes sexual indulgence must be prepared to accept and provide for the resulting offspring.

As long as there is the possibility of pregnancy, we must also face the problem of abortion. Despite the feminist movement, there has been little change in the position of women. It is still usually the woman who must make the decision on having an abortion, placing the child for adoption, or keeping the child born out of wedlock and trying to care for it herself. An abortion must be successful, because the baby that survives will have great difficulty in forming a relationship with its mother and probably with other people throughout life, because such a baby knows, deep in the unconscious, that it lives with its potential murderer. Properly done, a successful abortion is less harmful, because the soul that would have come will just have to find another channel.

Today's sentimentality about unborn babies is not even humane if no consideration is given to what the unborn child's life is going to be like. If it is not possible for a baby to grow into a healthy happy being, the sentimentality that's shown in trying to save it has little worth. A life with no future is no life. Those who make the judgment that abortion is wrong must take responsibility for finding a way to help make these new lives worth living.

Within a marriage, the taste for gratifying the instincts—which may already have produced children—will probably last only until the desire for new experiences arises. The desire may be sexual, or in men simply for powerful challenges that the relationship cannot provide. These desires for challenge are today matched in women who feel torn between successful careers and motherhood. A woman who may suddenly hear the striking of the biological clock and answer to it instinctively at the age of thirty-five or forty, may soon have regrets and find herself surprised, perhaps even angry, that motherhood has not fulfilled what it seemed to promise. Men often crave a son, and when he is born they are overjoyed, considering themselves lucky, even blessed. But as the son grows and approaches physical maturity, the father becomes aware that another strong power is now in competition with him.[2] Fatherhood also does not always live up to expectations.[3]

The old traditions, which provided the guidelines for what we could expect from life, have broken down considerably. Living now is like exploring new territory, so any step or decision we make will have to be carefully thought through. We are writing the script of our life, and we will be able to blame no one but ourselves for its outcome. However, this does give us an opportunity to be free from outmoded restrictions that prevent us from realizing our potential. But if we wish to expand our consciousness, we must realize that every pregnancy, every child postpones by at least eighteen years the intense work that is required to reach our spiritual goal. Each child presents an obligation that we must fulfill.

Most couples never compare the ever-increasing responsibility of rearing children with the few moments of sexual pleasure that lead to their birth. The classic fairy tale of Hansel and Gretel, sent off into the woods with only a little food in the hope they would become lost and perish, all too frequently represents the parents' attitude. Until recent times the very wealthy farmed their babies out to wet nurses, because they didn't consider children at such an age to be real members of the family. Children are often sent away from home as soon as they have finished high school, perhaps with a little money for college entrance fees, in the hope that they will get lost in their own interests and cease to be a burden or concern for their parents. Many children are abandoned by one or both parents long before they reach even that stage of maturity.

Few parents educate their children about marriage. Those who are really concerned about them will teach their children to look for character in the person they might marry, and to bring quality into their lives. Parents who have made a mistake must warn the child not to do the same, rather than allow pride to prevent them from admitting failure.

To love a child is to prepare it for life.

NOTES

[1]In a series of books, Swiss psychoanalyst, Alice Miller, has shown how parents need and use children to fulfill their own egotistic wishes, and the devastating effect this has on children and on the adults they become. Some of her books are included in the Bibliography.

[2]In his book, *Iron John,* Robert Bly encourages men to turn from competing with one another—being warriors and enemies—and instead to become friends. See Robert Bly, *Iron John* (New York: Addison-Wesley Publishing Company, Inc., 1990). But even the most companionable man cannot give the comfort that a woman can. If a man cannot give a woman a place in his life, he deprives himself of true companionship and comfort.

[3]Arthur Coleman and Libby Coleman, "Coming of Age: Alienation and Ambivalence." Chapter 8 in *The Father: Mythology and Changing Roles* (Wilmette, IL: Chiron Publications, 1988), 88–90.

Samuel Osherson, "Unspoken Debts: Men's Struggle to Separate from Father." Chapter 1 in *Finding Our Fathers: How a Man's Life is Shaped by His Father* (New York: Fawcett Columbine, 1986), 43–44.

No ghosts in my subconscious.
Pride is guarding the door,
preventing exit of the thieves
robbing me of liberation.
What am I so afraid of?
Very young, suffering and rejection
was the daily bread.
How can I take more?
A woman surviving in a man's world
has to be charming,
catty, and deceitful,
hiding true feelings of pain.
Don't be a victim of self-deception.
It is better to be with truth in hell
than with lies in heaven.

8 *Divorce*

THE MOST CRITICAL TIME in a marriage is around the ten-year period. In many situations the problem period starts a little before and runs a little beyond the ten years. If marital problems have been left unattended they will end in divorce. It is therefore important for any couple who are married, or for those who intend to get married, to take this into consideration and decide that they will make no decision at that time.

We can observe the cycles of our life even in daily living. It is helpful to chart these cycles by making a "mood-meter" each day, and so eliminate faulty decisions made at a low point in the cycle, which are usually emotional and unreasonable. By understanding ourselves in this way, we can avoid many problems in our relationships with others.

Residents of monasteries and ashrams experience the same cycles. If people who go to a spiritual community stay for three weeks, they often stay for three months. If they last a little more than three months, they are able to stay for two years. If they outlast the two-year cycle, they can probably remain until the ten-year period. After that, no other cycles have been observed. These observations very likely apply to a marriage relationship also, and it may be helpful to watch for them.

Couples often decide to divorce during one of these critical times, causing great upheaval for the whole family. Several questions arise: What was the motivation for getting married? Are the children unaffected in this battle between the sexes? If we cannot love, can we at least practice consideration? How much value do we put on human life in general, and our own offspring in particular? If the common idea that "love is sex and sex is love" was seriously considered, and the distinction made, children would never be pawns between the warring partners in a divorce.

I have sometimes said to people, "So you are tired of your spouse. You have found someone else who gives you attention and flattery, and there is perhaps a strong desire for sexual interaction, so you are now seeking a divorce that will make your children fatherless (or motherless). Have you considered the influences of your action on their development, that you are making them potential clients for psychotherapy later in their lives?"

The clever mind comes up with many explanations: the new father or mother will take care of the children and be good to them. But the children are rarely asked about *their* feelings. Children are innocent of their parents' difficulties but, by the perverse reasoning of the parents, they are thrown into circumstances that they are expected to be wise enough to understand and willing to go along with, denying their own needs.

Yet many fathers and mothers say they cannot pursue their own self-development because they cannot take time away from the home and family; they are too busy. They say they need a divorce to have the time for self-development. It would be very helpful for those parents to think about what they mean by the word *love*, because people who establish values in their lives, such as love, *are* doing something about their development, and it will show in the care they give their children.

Both partners have to realize that, after a divorce, a new romantic interest could mean that they would not be living their lives alone after all, and that these new relationships may be even less satisfying than the original ones.

What has changed in relationships that were supposed to be all love? What *is* love? Have you learned from a relationship, even if you have been unable to admit your part in the problems?

A new relationship may benefit you if you have learned from the marriage that has ended. All experiences are meant to help us along the path of evolution and, if we accept them as challenges, they can help us develop our individual consciousness.

After their grieving period has ended, many divorced women have become used to this different life of singleness, and have enjoyed a greater freedom than they had ever before known.[1] The trauma of divorce forced them to look at their emotional freedom and to realize how sex enslaves. Even the woman who is not pressed by sexual desires plays up to her man because his desire for her has become a measure of how much he loves her and cares for her.

The man may not go out of his way to have an extramarital relationship or to seek a new spouse, but he is attracted through his eyes and may become a victim to his senses and to his sexual drive. The female body, beautiful in itself, has been abused by the way it has been used in pictures and advertising for the purpose of stimulating men.

For the couple who feel divorce is unavoidable, if they can part as friends there will be no karmic repercussions. If they cannot do that, they will have to meet many times, through many lifetimes, until they have worked out their problems. To take revenge, act with bitterness, or make the situation a battlefield is wrong, because it is never only one partner who is at fault; there is an interaction and a stimulation to action from each to the other.

It would be better to make a friendship of the relationship *now,* and to do it while neither is involved with another person. Once one marriage partner becomes intimately involved with someone else, there is immediately a different flavor; the man now wants to keep more money for the new wife or new family; the woman thinks that all her problems will be solved because the new man will do what the old one did not. That, of course, is seldom the case.[2]

If you make an effort to understand that your partner comes from a very different place and has been formed by a different background, that will help to bring friendship into the relationship and enhance it, even though you plan to divorce. It will also aid your personal development, which is absolutely necessary even to live in peace and harmony with yourself.[3]

Truly concerned parents who feel divorce is inevitable, might realize that it would be better that they stay together until the children are grown. A husband, for example, could tell his wife, "I feel that I have nothing to give to you, and that you are not able to give anything to me. But we will stay together for the sake of the children. In the meantime, I am willing to pay for your education or training so that you will be in a good economic position when we decide to separate, because I may marry again." This approach has worked very well for some couples, and in fact when a woman develops herself, she gains not only self-respect, but also the respect of her husband.

By the time the children are seventeen, eighteen, or nineteen they will understand that sometimes relationships do break down. The parents will have fulfilled the obligation they took on in having children, and if they are wise, will have used this time to make themselves better people—more patient, less opinionated, less concerned with domination. This preparation will improve their lives in the future, regardless of what direction they choose.

It is possible to establish quality in any marriage by thinking deeply, by planning, and writing down all thoughts on the course you envision your life might take. But if your happiness has been bound up too much in children and family life, then when the children have all grown and taken their lives into their own hands, you will be shattered and will need an understanding partner. This is perhaps the time for husband and wife to explore together what other purpose there may be in life. If the idea of striving for Higher Consciousness is not acceptable to either of you, then ideals and ethics, or searching for wisdom, may provide your direction. Each of you has to seek fulfillment in life in your own way. The power of choice in relationships is tremendously important.

If you and your partner have been best friends, then the one who cannot follow the other's steps toward Higher Consciousness may sit back and wait, and in the meantime find other fulfilling activities. When one is developing a clearer contact with one's Higher Self, there may be a time of over-individualization, but for the one who strives for awareness this will be only temporary. In taking yourself out of the crowd, to do and live what you feel to be right and true, it might be necessary to go to this extreme, but it is a passing phase. A divorce is not always the answer, but if it is necessary, it should be done with no hard feelings, and with the knowledge that both of you have given to the other what you could.

The one who has recognized the spiritual path to be right for him- or herself must not allow the other to determine that it be given up. Such an individual might have to tell the partner that he or she has changed, that it is no longer possible to be the same man or woman who entered into the marriage. Sometimes these problems come to test the sincerity of your spiritual pursuit. There are many tests when one enters this path.

For the person who is on the spiritual path and who has achieved the union of the male and female within, there can be great psychological problems in living with a partner who is not interested in evolving spiritually. The relationship has to take a different form, either by agreement or through separation. There can be difficulties in finding a meeting ground, and the person who wishes to cater only to higher values will be unhappy with one who seeks the gratification of lower instincts. In such a case, it would be very difficult for partners to bring out the best in each other, and divorce might be the only solution.

Where your mind is, there your heart is also. If your mind is on Cosmic Consciousness, you must realize that in pursuing that goal you are obliged to give it your time and attention. Remember that *Yoga* means to join, like two oxen in a yoke, individual consciousness and Cosmic Consciousness.

Find out how urgent, how pressing, how intense is your goal of Cosmic Consciousness before making the decision to leave your partner. You should follow this path only when you are sure that following it is so important that, even if it cost your life, you would be willing to give it. Otherwise there is a danger that you will not become a fully realized yogi or yogini who has achieved Cosmic Consciousness, nor will you be fully living a worthwhile life in the world.

You will put yourself between two chairs. This is what is meant by the danger in Yoga. Let your intuition make the decision, rather than your ego.

What makes a person become interested in spiritual life? Sometimes it is only a woman's boredom with motherhood, or a man's desire to escape his obligations. But everyone must do his or her duty; one cannot develop at the expense of others. Swami Sivananda did not approve of leaving the family for spiritual life; he said that the family is a good preparation, "the battlefield of the *Gita*."[4] Once we have won our battles, the Divine creates a situation that makes it possible for us to pursue what we desire without causing the pain of breaking up a family. In the meantime, those who are still married, with children, can train themselves, prepare themselves. That will benefit the children and set them a good example for living a spiritual life themselves.

NOTES

[1]Margaret Adams. *Single Blessedness* (New York: Basic Books, Inc., 1976), 15.

[2]Making a friendship of the relationship may also help prevent the widespread defaulting on child support payments which grows out of the anger between the spouses.

[3]Gail Sheehy, *Passages: Predictable Crises of Adult Life* (New York: E. P. Dutton & Co., Ltd., 1976), 302.

[4]For elaboration on the *Bhagavad Gita,* see Chapter 11.

The cosmic dance—
in each life a different costume,
variation of steps in a new rhythm.
Speech of many tongues lost
in turning of the cosmic clock.

Have I lived before?
Memory is veiled in fog.
Grace a gift to forget—relief,
pain lessened. Gentle mist
moistens—some images
are soon washed away again,
lost in time. My identity is murky,
to say the least. Who am I to profess
to know? Maybe Light, manifest in
many shapes and forms. How many
names did this "I" answer to?
Each life full of challenges and links
in the chain of evolution.
Thoughts arise powerfully.
I am smaller than a grain of sand,
a star in the universe.

9 *Karma*

WHEN ATTAINING THE GOAL of Cosmic Consciousness has become acutely important for us, we have to consider the place of sex, love, and marriage in our lives. It is important to understand that the intensity of our desires plays a deciding factor in rebirth. Each life is a repetition of pleasure and pain. The pain and suffering usually outweigh the pleasures, so if we were to give this some serious thought we might realize it would be preferable to be relieved of rebirth.

Within each cycle of birth and rebirth it is possible to achieve the goal of Liberation. Anyone who achieves this purpose becomes an excellent being, a Bodhisattva, or, in Christian terms, a messenger of God functioning under the Divine Law, incapable of wrongdoing. The life of a such a person is dedicated exclusively to pure, perfect, compassionate actions to help others achieve the same goal. (Purity and perfection are not to be understood in the common moral sense, but rather within the Divine Law.)

But if we lapse into greed and selfish gratification, the Divine, by whatever name, demonstrates a love of such great compassion that, life after life, we are given another chance to undo our mistakes. Human beings have seen their gods as wrathful, vengeful, and fear-inspiring, but we now have a fuller grasp of the Divine because at this stage of development we have come of age and have grown in understanding.

The saints of both sexes had marvelous visions of Jesus, who epitomized for them the perfection of the Most High, but strangely enough they were also assailed by destructive forces that they called Satan. Satan is not some supernatural creature, but rather the personification of negative characteristics and tendencies in us. We can rightfully be called a demon, for example, if our greed has imposed pain and suffering on others. By accepting that God is within, we must also accept the opposite—Satan (or the demon).

This may be the place to remind ourselves that the Power (or Energy within) is neutral. How the Power is used is the awesome responsibility of each one of us. To give an illustration, everyone has the power to think, and that power is neutral, but we are each responsible for our thoughts and the actions that follow.

The kingdom of God within gives us the ability to be a blessing to all; to be a demon is to be a curse to all. Between those two extremes there is a scale as wide as the arc of a rainbow, and as multicolored as its subtle shadings. Ma-chig-lag,[1] who lived at the time of the Tibetan, Milarepa, taught her devotees that a demon is anybody who keeps you from fulfilling the purpose for which you took birth, even a loving parent who tries to tie you to tradition and duty.

Even if we have been born in humble surroundings, each of us can become either a saint or a demon. The purpose of life is the same for both—to seek Liberation. We can become a demon of self-gratification, even a criminal, but the evil person will also be given a chance to achieve the sublime goal.

In many lifetimes we have suffered because of karma.[2] Even a slight understanding of the retribution of karma shows that it can be compared to punishment or reward. However, karma offers us the opportunity to undo our mistakes and learn our lessons by accepting the challenges that come in life. Cause and effect need to be well understood. Over-simplification is tempting, but confusing, and finally frustrating. No definite or absolute statements can be made, because all depends on our individual awareness. We have the opportunity to undo bad actions and, by exercising proper choice and discrimination, we can increase our good actions. In the process we gain more insights, which help in making better choices in the future, recognizing that we can indeed become masters of our own destiny.

The practicing yogi or yogini accepts this karmic law of retribution, and is goaded on to meditation, possibly even to embracing asceticism, in an effort to prevent greed from again taking the upper hand. The monkey ego that tries to take the throne in the kingdom of wisdom has to be removed. Our essence will then be allowed to come to the foreground, and the personality aspects of the ego, that had previously been allowed to interfere and control, will be slowly dispersed.

Our effort to exercise restraint does not go unrewarded. The reward may be peace of mind, inner happiness, a state of bliss. Even if we experience those states only momentarily, the moments will gradually lengthen, and the times of unhappiness and of suffering will shorten. As we apply what we have learned in our attempt to gain self-mastery, we acquire the important tools of skill and discrimination.

Gods and demons, good and bad within each of us, are part of the same unit. The mind can move very quickly from one extreme to the other. Love and hate dwell together. The functioning of these opposite forces can be seen in many lovely stories and poems that illustrate the human condition. In a similar way, the gods and goddesses show us our destiny, symbolizing the innate powers that we can use to elevate ourselves.

Challenges refused and lessons not learned must be repeated; we are given another chance. That is karma; that is the process of evolution by which we reach our potential, the stage of Liberation. We can increase our intelligence and intuition only by our own effort, and our understanding of Cosmic Intelligence is the measure of our success.

The war that goes on between good and evil, gods and demons within us, is reflected in our actions in daily life, and in each millennium has its own effects. When the Divine Forces take on a manifestation, as we can see in the stories about Vishnu,[3] it becomes clear that the Cosmic Intelligence does not remain as indifferent as we might think. Vishnu, the god aspect of preservation, interferes and intervenes in human destiny. In yogic life this can be called factor x, the unknown, because none of us, of any race, can ever know every paragraph of our life's history.

A human life is but a second in the clock of eternity. In the same way that we cannot know all the factors in a human life, no one can be absolutely certain about results in sciences like astronomy or physics, even though data have been collected over many centuries, through numerous experiments and painstaking research. Even a very advanced person cannot be certain of knowing all the factors. There are no absolutes, there is no final truth. That is difficult to live with as long as we believe that truth has a beginning and an end. The only thing we can do is to accept the facts in our life, and they can be cruel.

Throughout the whole construct of many human lives, the level of understanding in each life becomes the foundation from which we start again. When building a house, making a good foundation assures the builder of straight walls and a roof that will not collapse, but will stand up in all sorts of weather, under all sorts of pressures. Similarly, when the foundation of our lives is solid, we are assured of right action. It is when the intellect becomes impatient and wants to leap ahead, or indulges in vanity and pride, that wrong action takes place because discrimination has been lost.

One result of such intellectual indulgence is the temptation, when people first become interested in past lives and reincarnation, to become intrigued by some historical figure—an important king, queen, or priest, for example—to the point of claiming to have been this person in a past life. However, the question should then be asked, Why am I only very ordinary in this life? Did I misuse my power when I held that important position?

But what does this mean for the aspirant who has no recollection of the many past lives that have gone before? There are some practical ways to lighten the burden of misdeeds and wrongdoing. First of all, look into the wrongs you know you have committed in this life. Some events will come into your mind first: you have deceived somebody, you have been dishonest, you have pretended to love someone when you did not. Then you might realize that you have swept the worst things under the carpet, so it takes effort to remember them. To balance each negative action that you recall, you can put the person involved into the Light,[4] or do some other spiritual practice, with the thought that the light of understanding and awareness will become active in that person's life, as well as in your own.

By making this conscious effort to atone for your wrongdoing, you will develop discrimination and keen observation in your own life. This can prevent you from making the same mistakes over and over, and help you to balance your own karmic record.

Discrimination will also help you to realize that, as you have hurt others unintentionally, so also some hurts may have been done to you without intent, and may indeed have only inconvenienced you. The next step then is to be able to forgive everything that has been done to you: "I will make an effort to forgive anyone who has hurt me, and I ask in return to be forgiven in the same proportion." That intention and the request you make of the Intelligence that is behind all karma, all life, and the creation of life, will lighten your burden, as long as you are serious about your decision, and set aside time for that purpose.

To forgive means that you free anyone from having to be reborn to mend the problems, the difficulties, and the pain that you have experienced because of them. You can forgive by trying to understand. The forgiveness and even the mercy that you need for yourself, you must also be able to give to others. Forgiveness is inexorably bound up with the karmic condition, and even though it may be a long time before you can forgive and forget, your consistent use of a spiritual practice for this purpose shows your goodwill and sincerity. Eventually the many good actions of that individual will come to the forefront of your memory, eradicating the hurt.

When a marriage is in danger, the only way of avoiding karmic retribution is to part as friends, realizing and admitting to each other, "I have nothing to give to you, and I am unable to receive from you." But strife, hatred, and strong feelings of revenge point to ignorance, because it takes two to quarrel. Also, it would be wise to remember that if there are children there will be "instant karma" in their lives. You must consider the effects on them if you seek a new relationship after parting from your spouse.

We often take steps toward a relationship when we are immature, when our feelings, attractions, and strong desires have not been substantiated. It is difficult to be truthful and to admit that for certain conveniences and gratification, we have entered relationships that, if only we had been willing to see, showed signs of decay as soon as they began.

The Chinese symbol of the yin-yang makes it clear that even if everything is quite perfect (a large white field), within it there is already a seed of the dark, while the opposite (a dark field) shows a white seed very prominently. Nothing is absolutely perfect, but neither is anything absolutely bad.

It has taken millions of years to create the kind of brain that can house the essence of consciousness that we have today. We must make the best use of our intelligence and understanding, however limited, to bring this cycle of life to completion in the best way we are able.

NOTES

[1]Ma-chig-lag achieved fame in the twelfth century. She was a disciple of Dam-pa Sang-Gye. For more information on Ma-chig-lag see George N. Roerich, *The Blue Annals* (Delhi: Motilal Banarsidass, 1979), 239, 982–83.

[2]"Karma means action; also the law of action and reaction, cause and effect. In Indian religions and philosophy Karma is the law of conservation of moral values, of merits and demerits of action. A man at any time is the sum-total of the results of his previous thoughts and acts, and at every moment is the builder of his future." Judith M. Tyberg, *The Language of the Gods: Sanskrit Keys to India's Wisdom* (Los Angeles: East-West Cultural Center, 1970), 6.

[3]H. H. Wilson, trans., *The Visnu Puranas* (Delhi: Nag Publishers, 1980).

[4]The Divine Light Invocation is a spiritual practice I was given in India. See Swami Sivananda Radha, *The Divine Light Invocation* (Palo Alto, CA: Timeless Books, 1990).

To find the entrance
to the hidden place
will demand mental acrobatics,
taking risks, destroying concepts
and unproven beliefs,
conquering fear of falling
from the rainbow into the abyss.

Remember, others before you
have done it, and did walk the rainbow,
their search sincere, their longing great.
The loving desire gave them strength.

Finally, lifetimes were
not wasted anymore.
The decision made is
crowned by a blessing.
The Pearl of Great Price is won.

10 *Divine Union*

IN MOST RELIGIONS there is the belief that humanity has fallen from its divine source. In the Judeo-Christian and Muslim traditions, when Adam and Eve had eaten from the Tree of Knowledge, they experienced shame in their difference and they covered themselves. Stories from other traditions also indicate this recognition that sex is a factor that must be dealt with.

Throughout the Puranas[1] and in the *Mahabharata,*[2] fire and water, male and female are represented as opposing forces. The gods and goddesses seem to reflect the problems of human life in their Cosmic Play.[3] They are the divine aspects of human beings, displaying life cycles that include periods of sexuality as well as celibacy. The need to create progeny is the motivating force in this Cosmic Play; the lack of progeny is considered a curse.

Various traditional texts reflect the purpose of sexual love. This purpose is expressed in a number of ways: it relates not only to sex, they say, but also to food and the reproductive forces of the body—with proper food the eggs or sperm are produced. We have known the psychological as well as the physical value of food since ancient times. Putting food into the baby's mouth is the mother's most tangible expression of her love and care. The husband's putting food into his wife's mouth, or the wife into her husband's, the sharing of one's favorite tasty, delicious eatables is a common way of showing affection.

In the love affairs of the gods and goddesses, intercourse is preceded by a gorgeous meal. But as we have seen in the story of Shiva and Parvati, the fulfillment of sexual desire leads to celibacy and, in the chain of cause and effect, celibacy builds the desire for fulfillment.[4] Excessive attention either to sexual love or celibacy leads to neglect of other duties.

Perhaps here we find the reason in mythology for the curse when the gods have no progeny: creation must be continued. However, the activity of the sexual energy, the creative force, must be balanced with celibacy. These two forces of powerful energy are like fiery horses that must be reined in, controlled, and directed. The Puranas tell us that Shiva was warned by the gods about his excesses, which symbolically mean his creative *and* his ascetic excesses. If he did not stop creating there would be too many mouths to feed. At other times, Shiva was urged to stop his *tapas* (austerity), to end his restraint and meditation so that creation would not die out—the paradox of the creative forces.

When the goddesses took to the tapas of celibacy, the gods urged Shiva to apply force, because emotions and love, fruit and vegetables are needed as well as music, joy, and laughter, so that the dance of life will continue. Then the gods incited Shiva to perform "The Dance of Bliss," and thereby distract the goddesses from their tapas since they were neglecting their duties of creation.

Celibacy, as much as sexuality, poses a threat when it is excessive. Control of all excesses guarantees balance. In certain religions, the prostitute serves as an example of the need for balance, as the ancient texts have recorded. One prostitute became a disciple of Jesus, and another a most devoted follower of the Buddha. It seems that by turning one focus into another (in this case, sexual focus into spiritual) the woman becomes aware of choices she had previously not known. These stories point out to women that they have a right to make choices, and urge them to do so.

In Yoga, in order to build a bridge between the spiritual and the carnal, the *Kama Sutra*s were instituted to keep a man and a woman together for a lifetime. This Yoga, called Maithuna,[5] is especially for married couples.

The *Kama Sutra*s offer a variety and a wealth of detail covering sexual love that has not been expressed in any other culture, and they always kept intact one spiritual law—the law of ahimsa. *Ahimsa* means "non-injury to oneself and others." Of course, there is a very fine line between refraining from harming others and the natural tendency toward self-protection, which can serve as an excuse for selfish actions that would indeed harm the other.

In Maithuna Yoga certain rituals have been established for the householder. This is in the tradition of *ashrama*, which means "the four stages of life." The first twenty-five years of one's life are for learning, the next twenty-five for living the life of a householder, the third twenty-five for studying with a Guru, and the last twenty-five being a Guru oneself. By following this Yoga householders can be prepared for more intense spiritual practice when their time comes, which is usually around the age of fifty. By that time they should be finished with the family and with sex.

For a married couple with children, the instructions from the *Kama Sutra*s ensure the happiness they are looking for and the opportunity to develop greater tenderness, love, and concern for each other. Under such circumstances, instincts have to take last place.

Without the benefits of a system like Maithuna, it may be difficult in our society for those who are married to achieve Higher Consciousness, but it is not impossible. To accomplish this takes extraordinary persons, partners who are emotionally independent, and who will not focus all their attention and energy on each other.

In this day and age when sex is glorified, couples who have a poor sexual relationship are often regarded as crippled, despite the fact that they may live together harmoniously, be very good friends, and have a great understanding for each other. Although this may be considered a disadvantage from the point of view of modern psychology, it may be beneficial for their spiritual development. If neither one has much interest in sex, it may actually mean that they have overcome one of the greatest obstacles to Higher Consciousness.

No relationship can be so fulfilling that it will replace the search for the Higher Self. Deep within, we know that we are strangers on earth, that we are a bridge between two worlds, and even though this knowledge may not be in our conscious mind, it is so rooted in the unconscious that it determines many of our actions. And although everyone looks for companionship, each one of us has to learn to stand alone. We become aware of this separateness when we try to share an emotional response with someone, even someone to whom we feel very close. We can view the same sunset with another person, be moved by the glory of the colors, but when we try to express our reactions we realize that the experience has been quite different for each of us. To an even greater extent, we must accept loneliness in our search for Cosmic Consciousness.

From a yogic point of view all sex, all self-gratification, however it is expressed, must go, because at the highest level the goal we desire to achieve is the Divine Union between our individual consciousness and Cosmic Consciousness.

In order to overcome the influence of our physical senses and their continuous demands, to become free of them, we need to practice increasing discipline. Unpleasant though this may be to modern people, without it we continue to create a world of disappointment and pain. The needs of the body are insatiable, and we have wasted thousands of births trying to fulfill them. At some time we must make a conscious decision to stop listening to the body's cries, and recognize that they are hindering our liberation from the wheel of life and death.

Sex is a tremendous force and it can be used in many ways. Each of us must choose what we will do with the creativity that is bound up with sex. This creativity can be channeled. Any artist knows that each new composition is a painful birth, with the agony of trying to reproduce what the inner eye sees, or what the inner ear hears. Through art a creative idea can be expressed, reaching its highest form when it has been dedicated to a spiritual purpose. We have only to remember the beautiful temples and cathedrals that have been built and decorated in glorification of the Divine Power.

Many artists, when they are creating, are not interested in sex. They do not wish to be bound to any expression of sexual energy, which they would rather direct to their artistic creation. The great dancer, Anna Pavlova, fell in love and married, but when she found that her performance was suffering, she divorced her husband. She needed all her energy for dance. A great deal of energy is exerted in sexual activities. In business the young man who is still caught in scheming to fulfill his sexual pleasures will not advance as quickly as the one who directs his energies toward the aims of the company. The same is true of the scientist in the laboratory. When the mind is concentrated unswervingly on the work, when one is interested in nothing else, all energy goes toward the goal.

The human body is capable of a great range of expression and experience, from very gross perceptions and actions to those of the highest subtlety. The sexual energy that we use mostly for self-gratification can be rechannelled to develop and refine the spiritual potential of the physical body. Through yogic exercises and practices that help refine the body—such as concentration, meditation, or Hatha Yoga—we can discover that it is capable of becoming a highly sensitive spiritual instrument.

The sexual force is part of that mysterious force, Kundalini, which Gopi Krishna[6] calls "man's evolutionary energy." It is available to all. It is every individual's birthright. That potential is within each of us. The only difference among us is whether or not we realize its presence.

Dr. von Urban, a sexologist who lived for three years in India, has written about the exchange of electrical energy between partners during sexual intercourse.[7] When the relationship is balanced, and the sexual expression is 50:50, this energy is neutralized in each other. However, if sex is more of a biological function, repetition increases the lack of balance, and the marriage is affected adversely.

The couple on the spiritual path who precede their sexual togetherness by meditation and an expression of concern for each other, experience sexual bliss that can indeed be a foretaste of the bliss that lies ahead, an assurance of the spiritual heights in which there is a different oneness.

Tantra Yoga,[8] which at one time did create extraordinary beings, is a system in which dedicated tantrikas undertake rigorous practices to transform themselves and achieve the union of the two selves within. In traditional Tantra Yoga the Guru selects a male and female who are at a similar level of development. It is not important that they be attracted to each other; they are selected for their ability to control their sexual energy. At this level of development it is true bliss that they desire, not just the physical pleasure that is over quickly.

In his book *The Tantric View of Life*, Herbert Guenther speaks of the male and female within the same body.[9] It is the union of these two selves that is the first purpose of the tantric yogi. However, as the oral tradition was passed down through the generations, the practical application of the practices of Tantra Yoga was interpreted according to the desires of those who practiced. This seems to be an attribute of human nature. When degeneration of a system has reached a certain point, it is difficult to recognize its original intent and goal.

Tantric yogis who permit sexual indulgence and what is usually termed "a good life" can do so only at the cost of their female counterparts, and the offspring who are the possible outcome of such indulgence. Unfortunately, some books show physical positions for sexual pleasure, calling it Tantra Yoga.[10]

The goal that the follower of the tantric path aims for is symbolized by the *vajra*, the diamond that reflects the many colors of life. The diamond is the hardest stone to use for "cutting through." Opposing tendencies within must first be acknowledged. Then the goal is to become as hard as a diamond to cut through all obstacles in oneself, to recognize the power of the opposites, and to be aware that they may manifest either way, at any time.

Shining the light of understanding onto the facets of your own diamond can lead you to the Void, which does not mean "non-being," but rather "clarity of being." The transformation to that clarity of being is like the cutting and polishing of a rough diamond. As you observe the process, you will gain new insights. You will see each event in the light of logic and reason, recognize the interference of your emotions, and balance the inclinations of your desires against the goal you have set. In this way you transform the rough and dark abyss into the pure Light.

Seekers have taken many different paths to solve the problem of their sexual desires. One path favors exploiting sexual pleasures to the utmost. Another favors abstinence and asceticism. Those who have chosen asceticism as their path of sexuality are seldom understood by others. Their motivation for practicing abstinence or asceticism is often interpreted as fear of sex. It is true that some fear emotional entanglement or being an unsatisfactory partner, but they are exceptions. More likely they fear that something will be lost—that their path to Realization will be blocked by the responsibilities that come with offspring. Yogis who strive to achieve the goal of expanded consciousness have the same single-pointedness of mind as any artist. They choose celibacy in order to preserve their energy so they can attain that state.

The yogi or yogini who is dedicated to the goal of Cosmic Consciousness is swimming against the river of life. That seems to be cruel and demanding, and difficult to understand, but we must realize that we are in exile and have to make our way back to the country of our origin. It is as if we had emigrated from heaven down to earth and are struggling to return to heaven.[11]

If we are all truly divine beings, then we do not belong only here in the physical world, and we should not allow animal instincts to rule our lives. There is little difference between an animal and Animal-Man. The house of Animal-Man is simply a bigger nest, the children are the litter, and he goes out to hunt food, or earn dollars to buy the food and feed his family. In Man-Man, development toward consciousness brings a new perception of sex. It is not a matter of morals, but of understanding the Divine Law.

Let us assume that at one time we had those celestial bodies, and that there was no need for procreation[12] because we could recreate our own bodies by the power of the mind. That knowledge may still be deep within and provide the impetus for our search for a different union. Each of us is a bridge between the world of the physical, material self that seeks sexual expression, and that of the Higher Self where there can be a communication of souls that has no connection with sex.

Throughout our history we have had many strange thoughts. Have we created our ideas of immortality? It is my conviction that we cannot think of anything that does not already exist. If we originated in a different dimension, some of this memory may still linger deep within each one of us.

When the creation becomes independent of its creator, it takes its own course, like the cultures and empires that we have created. We also have taken our own course, having been created by the Divine Forces, then becoming independent of our source. But when we recognize that the Supreme Intelligence dances in the Self, then the mind stands in awe of its power and splendor, and acknowledges the Creator. The Dance of Life consists of steps of fierceness and destruction, as well as steps of swiftness, lightness, and elegance. We must dance a thousand of those steps before we reach the pinnacle of our own divinity. They are the dance of our evolution.

If we equate divinity with awareness, then perhaps we can say that the ideal is realized when Shiva and Shakti[13] dance together, when together the inner male and female dance the Dance of Life—Shiva, the great unfathomable creative power, and Shakti, all of creation.

When we have become divine through our own dance of life, we see the rainbow between the two worlds, and we understand our place in the universe. Yet we know the rainbow has no substance, and that we can perceive it only when our mind is in a certain specific condition. Although we look for permanence and dependability, myths of all ages point to fluidity. Life cannot be tied down to solid events within a permanent structure. Life is flow.

Metaphysical dimensions and awareness of cosmic powers continue to upset our rigid concepts and plans, making us fluid. The divine being knows in heart and mind that the Power that created the mind is beyond mind, and that each one of us, male and female, is the handmaiden of the Great Goddess, who is that power itself made manifest.

Notes

[1]Puranas: the legendary histories of ancient India, which are the principal Scriptures of Vaishnavism and Saivism.

[2]The *Mahabharata* is ". . . the great epic of the Bharatas of 220,000 lines divided into 12 books. It is a great collection of poetry consisting of legendary philosophical material worked into and around a central heroic narrative which portrays the struggles between the two Bharata families: evil-minded Kurus and the virtuous Pandavas." Judith M. Tyberg, *The Language of the Gods: Sanskrit Keys to India's Wisdom*, 2d ed. (Los Angeles: East-West Cultural Center, 1976), 100.

[3]"Because the gods are complete and therefore do not act according to pragmatic laws of cause and effect to fulfill this or that desire, their actions are called play. . . . The gods as players are revealed to act spontaneously, unpredictably, and sometimes tumultuously. To play is to be unfettered and unconditioned, to perform actions that are intrinsically satisfying: to sing, dance, and laugh." David R. Kinsley, *The Sword and the Flute* (Berkeley: University of California Press, 1977), 73-4.

[4]Wendy Doniger O'Flaherty, *Asceticism and Eroticism in the Mythology of Siva* (London: Oxford University Press, 1973), 4-6.

[5]Sir J. Woodroffe, *Shakti and Shakta* (London: Luzac, 1929), 578.

Alan W. Watts, *Nature, Man and Woman* (New York: Vantage Books, 1970), 161-62. "The general idea of Tantric maithuna, as of its Taoist counterpart, is that sexual love may be transformed into a type of worship in which the partners are, for each other, incarnations of the divine."

[6]Gopi Krishna, *Kundalini: The Evolutionary Energy in Man* (Berkeley: Shambhala Publications Inc., 1970).

[7]Rudolph von Urban, *Sex Perfection and Marital Happiness* (New York: The Dial Press, Inc., 1949), 78-126.

[8]Omar Garrison, *Tantra: The Yoga of Sex* (New York: The Julian Press, Inc., 1964), xv-xxviii. The Introduction gives a clear and lucid explanation of the philosophy and history of Tantra Yoga.

[9]Herbert Guenther, *The Tantric View of Life* (Berkeley: Shambhala Publications Inc., 1972), 98.

[10]There is also some misunderstanding about the function of Hatha Yoga and its relation to sex. I would like to quote from the *Hatha Yoga Pradipika* which says, "Teaching Hatha Yoga is solely for the attainment of Raja Yoga." The commentary says, "By using the word solely it is made plain that the object of practising Hatha Yoga is to prepare for Raja Yoga, not to obtain the siddhis, the psychic powers." And it is *not* for the purpose of increasing sexual energy.

Pancham Sinh, trans., *The Hatha Yoga Pradipika*, 3d ed. (New Delhi:

Munshiram Manoharlal Publishers, 1980), 61.

[11]Swami Sivananda Radha, *Kundalini Yoga for the West* (Spokane, WA: Timeless Books, 1978), 340.

[12]Matthew 22:30. "For in the resurrection they neither marry, nor are given in marriage, but are as the angels of God in heaven."

Alan W. Watts, *Nature, Man and Woman* (New York: Vantage Books, 1970), 152. Jesus told his disciples that there is neither marriage nor giving in marriage in heaven, meaning that heaven, the sacred sphere, stands above the social institutions of the earthly sphere.

[13]*Shakti* is a general term for energy manifest; *Parvati* is a more personalized term.

I stand by the pond,
look into its clear water,
remember little Krishna.
"Please, mother, let me see
the moon." Yasodha points
to the reflection in the water.

There is no moon now
but a face beautiful, gentle;
deep penetrating eyes
like dark suns
shining brightly. "Krishna,
what is this? Is it really You,
or a projection of my mind?
Your response to my longing
an assurance of your
everlasting presence?"
A white lotus swaying gently.
Memory externalized,
in blue onyx shimmering a single pearl.
"Krishna, they call you a thief.
You are a magician, too."

11 Symbols of Divinity

IN HINDU MYTHOLOGY the gods and goddesses embody the highest aspirations of men and women. The epic poem, the *Mahabharata,* expresses universal thoughts, sentiments, and emotions through the display of its characters' human strengths and weaknesses. It is the story of the struggle of humanity to understand and live by the Divine Law and, through its symbolism, the epic relates directly to the basic issues of sex, love, and marriage even today.

Krishna is the teacher in the *Bhagavad Gita* (which is part of the *Mahabharata),* and in India he is one of the gods who is seen as the connection by which the individual can relate to the cosmos. Krishna is known also as Gopala, a little boy, and as such he is attractive to many seekers.

One day Krishna's mother caught him eating earth, and punished him for his misbehavior. To her amazement, as he began to cry, suddenly she saw the whole cosmos in his mouth. Symbolically this shows his potential as a god, even while he was still displaying the characteristics of a little boy. Stories of Krishna as a child do not mean that God has to come of age, but that human beings have to evolve in their understanding of the Divine.

As he grew up, Gopala was sent to look after the cows, and spent much of his time teasing and playing with the *gopi*s, the milkmaids. He loved them all and they loved him, but the one he chose as his beloved was Radha. She represents individual consciousness, which is seeking to unite with Cosmic Consciousness, personified in Krishna.

When we set foot on the spiritual path, we have innocence and faith. Radha, the innocent lover of Krishna, has no pride. There is joy in love for its own sake, with no expectation that it will be rewarded. This joy is expressed particularly beautifully in the dance of Radha and Krishna. When finally Krishna singled out Radha and danced with her, he multiplied himself in the minds of the gopis. And so they enjoyed just being present—without jealousy, without possessiveness, without expectations—but each one also experienced that ecstatic Divine Union of Radha with Krishna.

One might ask, "Why should one see God as a romantic lover?" There is a very simple answer: Unless we have a love affair with the Divine that overrides all other desires and activities, we will never take steps toward consciousness.

In Indian painting, Krishna is usually portrayed as blue, the color of a dark thundercloud. Since no human race has skin of that color, this symbolizes that he is not a mortal lover.

Some experiences of physical union hint at a union of a much higher order, beyond anything to be achieved on the physical plane. In the actual climax of sexual union each individual loses consciousness of self for a few seconds. That union, on a higher level, is the meaning of Yoga—joining the individual consciousness with Cosmic Consciousness—and this is symbolized by Radha and Krishna. For the uninitiated that may be difficult to understand, but for the person who has the perception to penetrate the symbol deeply, and discover the underlying meaning, this is precisely what it means.

Many symbols are used in Indian painting and poetry. One of them is the lotus whose beautiful pure flower blooms above the water, but whose roots are embedded in the mud at the bottom of the pool. This implies that no matter under what muddy conditions we may have been born and have lived, each of us can produce the beautiful lotus of consciousness. This is important, because in speaking of love that is exceptional, we may be inclined to think of fairy-tale princes and princesses, or aristocrats with silken robes and glittering jewels. But Krishna's love is for a simple girl who tends the cows, and whose freshness and innocence are her priceless jewels.

Rain clouds can have a variety of meanings. Rain and lightning might seem to mean passionate love, the exciting embrace of lovers. But in Indian mythology, Krishna's color, dark blue as a rain cloud, symbolizes Divine Love, which to us is usually unknown, beyond the limitations of our minds. In contrast to modern life that is complicated and frustrating, in Divine Love we find the clarity of uncomplicated humble sincerity.

Clouds may also mean that in spiritual life we have to go through the darkness of unknowing in order that our faith may be strengthened. Faith is the guiding Light, but it is not always visible. Sometimes we feel caught in the rain where our vision is limited. But the lightning that pierces the cloud represents insights that light up and bring meaning to life, if only for a brief moment.

The symbolism is not a rigid one that can be locked up in a lexicon. It is alive, its meaning shifting, depending on our experience and understanding. As Westerners, we may be baffled by the symbolic meaning of Radha and Krishna's sexual embrace. But perhaps someone from India looking at the pictures of Christ on the cross might think that death was worshipped and that punishment was the main concern of the Christian, unless the meaning and the Light of Christ were understood.

Krishna has two aspects: the lover dancing with the milkmaids, expressing the innocence of Divine Love, and the Krishna of the *Bhagavad Gita,* a very different character, an enigma who seems to advocate death and destruction. But this, too, is symbolic of human development. At first, we believe without question. As time goes by, blind belief is no longer sufficient, and it has to be tested. That is the beginning of our maturity. When entering the spiritual realm we need time to develop. The spiritual baby encounters a different kind of life. Conflicts appear, and we must struggle to gain understanding. Krishna, the lover of Radha and the milkmaids, is also the stern teacher.

The *Bhagavad Gita,* in which Krishna's teachings are revealed, is part of the *Mahabharata,* which deals with the forces of good and evil, of attraction and repulsion, and shows the confusion and complexity they create. This epic could be considered India's Bible, and its story should be regarded symbolically. It is the story of two rival families that sprang from the same royal parents, each member of the family representing a human characteristic in an exaggerated way, in order to clearly convey the story's message.

Pandu and Dhritarashtra were royal brothers. Pandu became king and had five sons who were called the Pandavas. If we see the five sons as representing the five senses, we can understand their symbolic meaning. Each son can produce many children, just as each of our senses produces many results, and they affect the members of both the immediate and the related families.

Dhritarashtra, the head of the second family, was blind, representing the intentional blindness that is so common to many of us. This blindness is caused by emotions. Its numerous effects are symbolized by Dhritarashtra's one hundred sons, called the Kauravas.

When Pandu died, Dhritarashtra became king and brought up the two families together in the same court. The court is the whole earth, where there are people of diverse qualities and talents, with the same jealousies as those that arose from the rivalry between these two families. In the *Mahabharata* the jealousies originated from boyish contests, but jealousy, competition, and arrogance always have a deadly outcome. These deadly games of rivalry have been played since the beginning of time, and we play them still, with a surprising lack of awareness of how destructive they are. In fact, competition is highly advocated in the West today, both for men and for women.

The Pandavas were brave and intelligent, which kindled the Kauravas' hatred of them. But after the chief of the Pandavas used his intelligence to become a conqueror and claim the title "ruler of the world," stupidity took over and he lost everything—his kingdom, his brothers, even his wife—in a game of dice with the Kauravas. The five brothers and their wife, Draupadi, were banished into the forest for twelve years. Draupadi represents meditative, perceptive intuition that, through receptivity, can bring creative insights. The forest is dark, a good place to hide, but it also shuts off all other influences. One's ability to see is limited, and so the sense of hearing is heightened in order to detect danger. In the dark the sense of touch and of smell will be sharpened, as circumstances force one to use them. Thus the perception of neglected senses is increased.

We are told that the Pandavas remained in the forest for twelve years. Human life goes in cycles. There is an upward movement like a wave, bringing with it great enthusiasm, but then the wave recedes and there is a period of rest or an experience of despair, until the wave begins to rise again. Many of us can verify from our own experience that after a period of ten or twelve years the desire for another change arises. Monastic orders are aware of these cycles, and place the renewal of vows at the time when restlessness is beginning and can be directed. As already mentioned, it has been recognized that around the tenth year marital or family crises often occur. Professionals may find similar cycles in their work.

There is a basic duality within us that causes these cycles. One part—the physical—is satisfied with having food, shelter, warmth, and sex. The other part—the mental-emotional—is stimulated by the mind's creative ability that is rooted in imagination and desire. This duality is also present in the expressions of love and hate, peace and war, in the numerous opposing aspects that are represented by the one hundred sons of the blind king, Dhritarashtra.

In the *Bhagavad Gita* the battle between the two families provides the setting for the teachings of Lord Krishna. He is the charioteer of Arjuna, commander-in-chief of the Pandavas, who represents the confused human being. It takes a higher spirit, one of divine origin, to help us out of our confusion. This Cosmic Intelligence is personified by Krishna. He gives encouragement in the *Bhagavad Gita* by teaching that whatever knowledge and understanding we have gained in one lifetime is not lost, but will form the foundation for another.[1]

In the context of this book we cannot give the symbolic meaning of the entire epic, so we will confine ourselves to the basic principles. Social customs and traditions change from century to century, but the epics of all the nations of the world tell the same story of the complexities of the human family. The sophisticated Westerner may say that every age has had its gods and goddesses, and that over a period of time they have outlived their purpose and "died." But the human need for objects of devotion and aspiration can be seen today in the worship of rock musicians, and football or hockey stars, while the scientist has also assumed an almost god-like stature. In the *Gita* Lord Krishna promised that he will reincarnate whenever negative characteristics like greed and selfishness outweigh common sense and concern for others, and it appears that such are the conditions today.

Krishna gave his teachings to Arjuna, the prince. One might ask why Krishna does not bring his message to the poor, instead of to those who rule. But the masses are always impressed by the powerful or knowledgeable, and follow their example. Therefore, by teaching the leaders, Krishna urged them to set an example of honesty, mercy, and justice.

There are many choices for us to make in life, many challenges to be accepted. And even though much has been taught on the subject of evil, it has not yet been removed. No war ever saves the innocent, the afflicted, the sick, or the hungry, although the purpose of every war is said to be to rectify some injustice. The root of war is the temptation to act from a position of strength, to take revenge, to exploit, to increase power, to control, to enslave, to destroy. Yet side by side with the tyrants of war can be found individuals who perform heroic acts, control lower instincts, and express mercy, pity, concern for the welfare of others, even for the "enemy" who is conquered. Understanding and compassion are not attributes of the masses, but of a few who stand out from the masses, and whose extraordinary qualities are recognized. In the same way, the spiritual giants, the yogis or saints of any nation, are venerated. This is understandable because it is much more difficult to conquer oneself than to conquer a nation.

The conquering of all those aspects that gratify self becomes very subtle indeed. We bring with us into each life many memories and influences that we must eventually bring under control. For the yogis and yoginis who have decided upon enlightenment as their sublime goal, the self-mastery they attain will make them powerful. Yogis and yoginis are not limited to India or to any particular religion. They are those who seek Realization by a spiritual path, whether within a religion or not.

Let us return for a moment to the Pandavas. The five brothers had won a king's daughter, Draupadi, in a competition held amongst the elite young men who were acceptable to her parents. Draupadi was given to the winner as a reward. This serves to illustrate the low value given to women: because she was female, Draupadi was given to the winner of the contest as a prize, to become his bride.

On the spiritual level, the prize to be gained through self-mastery is union with the Higher Self. But on a human level this story shows that the respect and dignity, which is the right of every human being, was disregarded in the case of women, just as it is today. The inferior position of any female, even a princess, is determined at birth. The custom of trading or selling females into service or slavery has existed in many cultures throughout all ages.

The rich girl of today would still meet with great objections if she were to marry a poor man. In the past, marriages in the higher strata of society were controlled in a subtle way, even though they were not formally arranged by the parents. Well-to-do young ladies could only meet young men who were acceptable to the family as eligible bridegrooms. The bachelors were allowed sexual escapades, at least until it became time to marry, when they had to fall in with the traditions and rules of their society. The First and Second World Wars changed some of this, but the real changes took place only in recent decades, and resulted in greater freedom. But even today, to marry outside one's race or religion is frowned upon in some sectors of the population. We are too often astonished at the customs of other countries that in reality may differ only slightly from those of our own, where manipulation perhaps has just become more subtle. It is precisely this conditioning that has made the human female the lesser sex.[2]

The basic manifestation and manipulation of the senses that perceive the world can be seen symbolically in the one hundred sons of the blind king, Dhritarashtra. In this way the world is categorized and recorded in the logical sequence of history, but also in a most irrational way by the impact on us of our life's events. Love, sex, and marriage are the main driving forces in human life, and these often cause us to be as blind as the king.

The much admired characteristics of intellect, reasoning, and logic are not the only attributes of even the greatest scientific mind, because that mind belongs to a human being who is endowed with feelings, although this is often conveniently forgotten, since feelings are unacceptable to the intellect. If the main concern and energy have gone to the development of the intellect, the emotions and feelings will remain overlooked and unrefined. They may then erupt into sudden outbursts or depressions.

If we take the epics and Scriptures of the world and see them in relation to ourselves in our daily lives, through the many stages of our development, then we can recognize the wisdom that has come from the great minds, the seers, of all cultures. We do not need to struggle with the idea that the Scriptures are the direct word of God. We can understand this wisdom as having come from a human being who was capable, by self-discipline and self-mastery, of listening to the inner voice of God that today we call insights or intuitive perceptions. The genius emerges apparently from nowhere, appearing like a comet in the night skies, leaving behind a blazing trail. That blazing trail might be only the fragmentary memory left from moments of awareness. But we respond because modern people retain certain values derived from previously valued beliefs, even though they have been undermined by nagging doubts.

The wisdom that has come to us from the seers and geniuses shows that evolution has been an ongoing process. Although some people have seemed to evolve faster than others, this can perhaps be understood in regard to the six stages referred to earlier. Extraordinary people have become like gods in the minds of the simple, ignorant, or illiterate. The basis for such extraordinary achievement is concentration, contemplation, and awareness, and the ability to listen to the inner voice of intuition.

The yogi or yogini transcends ordinary knowledge and perceives knowledge that radiates from a higher source, which gives quite a different perspective to daily living. The yogin looks for a very different solution from Darwin's; the yogin looks for the evolution of consciousness. He or she will recognize the urgent need for cooperation with evolution, rather than the stubborn resistance that makes life so painful. The objective is to look into the purpose of life as far as one can see. The various divisions of Yoga all have the same goal— Liberation.

Over and over again it must be stated that it is essential to take one step at a time and keep under control the curiosity of the ego that wants to know the outcome beforehand. As long as we use the term *I,* saying, "I'm angry, or I need rest, or I have pain," we still need this individual concept of ourselves and should not attempt suddenly to dispose of ideas of self. To do so only complicates and delays understanding. These questions of the ego will answer themselves with greater clarity than any explanation could provide, as one nears that realm where all concepts finally vanish.

According to the Buddhist tradition, one has to have a consciousness that differs from the masses in order to approach that sublime realm. The Christian tradition tells us the same thing. Jesus' answer to the question, How shall we pray? was an example that everyone would understand. His prayer began, "Our Father," because the father was the ruling force in the family. To those who had been with him day after day for the three years of his ministry, he said, "The Kingdom of Heaven is within."[3] The disciples had to come from the realm of understanding of "I am, I eat, I see, I walk" to the knowledge of that kingdom within themselves.

How, then, can such perception be achieved? This is what reincarnation is all about. We have already seen how Lord Krishna expresses his love and concern for his creation and assures his beloved devotee, Don't worry. I will give you opportunities over and over. The body may drop away, but the essence that is you will maintain the memory.[4]

On the subject of reincarnation, we are given to understand through the *Gita* that when the desire is great enough for release from life, or from the possessiveness of the earth that holds us jealously, a higher birth will be possible and will assist us to cooperate with our evolution. Mind and intellect expand into greater awareness. Increased knowledge in each life then becomes like capital in a bank account on which interest can be drawn. If that knowledge is applied in daily living, the spiritual capital increases and becomes finally the wealth to procure that sublime end.

Krishna's flute is the instrument by which his devotees are lured back to their heavenly home. The melody of the music he plays is the call of God to those still wandering in the darkness. When Krishna plays the flute in Brindavan, the gopis' reaction is symbolic of our inner response—a deep longing for the Most High, even while engaged in the battle of life.

NOTES

[1]The *Bhagavad Gita* makes this clear in Chapter 6:

41. "Having attained to the worlds of the righteous, and having dwelt there for everlasting years, he who fell from Yoga is reborn in a house of the pure and wealthy.

42. "Or he is born in a family of even the wise Yogis; verily a birth like this is very difficult to obtain in this world.

43. "There he comes in touch with the knowledge acquired in his former body and strives more than before for perfection, O Arjuna."

[2]Girls from wealthy families even today are not encouraged to have careers, although they often receive fine educations at good private schools. Their main purpose is still often seen as making a suitable marriage.

[3]"But the Kingdom is within you and it is without you. If you (will) know yourselves, then you will be known and you will know that you are the sons of the Living Father." A. Guillaumont, trans., *The Gospel According to Thomas: Coptic Text Established and Translated* (New York: Harper & Row, 1959), 3.

[4]*Bhagavad Gita* 9:22: "To those men who worship Me alone, thinking of no other, to those ever-united, I secure which is not already possessed (Yoga) and preserve what they already possess."

9:31: "Soon he becomes righteous and attains eternal peace; O Arjuna, know thou for certain that my devotee is never destroyed."

Challenges have many roots.
Recognition is a must,
neglect is a poison,
rejection fatal.
Deficiency is not measured
by psychological investigation.
Understanding is helpful,
only a step to evolution.
Take courage and responsibility.
Don't escape into
intellectual shrewdness.

12 In the Divine Image

WHEN WE SEEK Higher Consciousness, when we have even an inkling of what the purpose of life is, our identification must be with awareness, consciousness, the inner Light, the inner Buddha or, as Jesus said, "the kingdom within." In a passage from the Gospel According to Thomas, Jesus told the disciples to tell people that they are born of Light, and that Light was born of itself.

Each of us, man or woman, must identify with the Light, because it is only by that identification that we can find our way. Achieving proper identification is part of the path of our evolution. So how do we start? With very tangible things. We begin by bringing quality into our daily life. While we may not be able to love everybody, we can at least be considerate, thinking that the Divine in me must recognize the Divine in the other. The woman must help bring out the best in the man; and he must do the same for her. Then a relationship between the two makes sense, and elevates it beyond the level of simply using each other.

The divine woman devotes herself completely to life and creation, as well as to loved ones, and her dedication can be recognized in the quality of the smallest of her acts, whether in her domestic life, her profession, or her personal life. But even the most important events of a woman's life—the first joys of love, the cry of her first-born—become insignificant when she attempts to define her relation to the universe. When she looks to the distant stars, outer space seems even more awesome than human tragedies. And the mysteries of the moon or the beauty of a sunset outweigh the greatest catastrophe.

Women tend to focus on their personal lives and relationships, to the exclusion of the broader perspective. But the divine woman has widened her horizon, and the small things of her life then fall into their proper place.

Women have had few models of other women to follow, but the way of life adopted by yoginis provides an example because they have achieved a clear understanding about the various aspects of life—birth and death, with all the shades between. Yoginis have cultivated sufficient interest in themselves to think for themselves, to expand their consciousness, and to gain emotional independence.

It is my hope that, after reading this book, some women will be encouraged to accept responsibility for their own lives, to take their rightful place in the world, and to become divine themselves. In doing so, they will not only help themselves and their families, but they will also free men from assuming that responsibility, and will inspire men also to think more deeply about the meaning of life, and their own path of evolution.

Women must also look at how they are assessed by their own sex as well as by men: What is a good woman, what is a bad woman? What is sexual freedom, and what is responsibility? What is independence, and what is interdependence? What is instinct? What is intuition? What is consideration, compassion, love?

I have already pointed out the differences between love, instinct, and emotional attachment. Once again, I urge women to really clarify these differences to themselves, on the gut level—no romancing, no covering up, but seeing the facts as they are and recognizing one great truth in Yoga: that truth indeed is cruel.

Today there are many organizations that try to help women, particularly those who are exposed to violence in their marriages. The leaders of such groups are unanimous in saying that women often have a fantasy about men and their relationship with them, and that women make the kind of demands for romance that have been described in love stories the world over.

It may help women's understanding to get involved in studying the history of their own sex,[1] but that in itself is no protection. Women have been pawns in the hands of the leaders of many nations; there is almost no country in the world where this has not taken place. But we usually point to other countries (particularly non-white), as if only they were capable of such actions.

Looking into prostitution in the past may throw some light on "the bad woman." In ages when women had no power whatsoever, men will have to take the responsibility for having created the bad woman. A bibliography has been included in this book for those who are interested in pursuing their reading of the history of male-female relationships.

The women's revolution now gives women a chance to take their lives into their own hands, and no longer allow men to use them for political bargaining, as they have in issues such as abortion. Women struggle today for the rights over their own bodies and over their own lives. They should not limit their struggle only to their exercise of power. Women must also explain to those who would wield power *over* them what emotional suicide is being demanded of them.

How many women were unwanted children themselves, and what was their suffering? Their stories are only beginning to be told, and it should be every woman's duty to be well-informed on such issues for her own sake. Does she want a baby because all women should be mothers? Is there truly any glory in motherhood, and how does that compare with the enormous responsibility of bringing a new life into the world?

The responsibility is clearly on each woman to decide between sex and celibacy. Many women have some understanding of the power becoming available to them and their need to use it properly, to take responsibility for their actions, and to avoid putting the blame on others.

If it seems cruel to look at the facts as they are, we must consider that when decisions are made in a romantic mood, full of hopes and wishful thinking, the breakdown that follows or the lack of fulfillment is much more cruel. A woman's decision to be with a man should not be made out of financial need, even less out of emotional need, because then neither one can trust the other.

We are still a long way from having women enjoy each other's company as much as they do men's, and respecting each other's perceptions, viewpoints, and tastes. The emotionally dependent woman strains to agree with her man because she thinks that otherwise problems will arise in their relationship. But she could choose to put the same effort into living beyond the crowd.

Is a woman "good" if she plays up to the hopes and wishes of a man? The so-called good woman is always comfortable, creates no waves, and upholds traditional concepts of purity and chastity. To guarantee that this concept is continued, girls have often been married at an unusually early age. And here again, let us look at the facts: this does not happen only in certain non-white or non-Western societies.

Misuse of the freedom given to us resulted in the punishment that was recorded symbolically in the Old Testament: we were thrown out of Paradise. It is not within the purpose of this book to tell you what your choice in sexual activity should be, because that would interfere with your ability to recognize that the power of choice is yours. The purpose is rather to help you to understand the course of evolution and to use freedom wisely. Maybe woman's evolution has finally become truly visible.

Would we have anything different to tell the men? What are the choices men must make? Instincts, the drive for procreation, and the tendency to turn that into pleasure are factors that limit men's power of choice. But among men, too, there are some who will choose to live a life of greater quality.

The divine man recognizes the divinity in himself and identifies with the Light in the other person. He is aware, considerate, and puts quality into life. He knows he has the power of choice and learns to use that power in a positive way, rather than negatively. He knows that he is not limited to being just a provider and gratifier, just to carrying out the garbage and bringing the money home.

The divine life can be very hard for a man. Male pride is a big obstacle. Men may not even be aware of what a big demon it is. When you love your pride, you cannot love anything else, not even your own children. That is why some swamis in India say they wish to be born a woman: because it is the only way they know to get humility and devotion.

Men's investment seems to be in power, control, and sex. The man who has any other interest is so much an outsider that he is not accepted by other men. But the door is open for a man, if he can just pull out of this herd instinct. He must choose to live beyond the crowd, not just to be competitively on top of it, but actually beyond it, outside its concerns and values. Though this can seem difficult, men are capable of great dedication.

It is also important for men to realize that perhaps they have never fully clarified how emotionally dependent they are upon women, nor have they realized that dependency prevents them from being themselves. Instead, they resent the dependency, and they blame women for it. In fact, as we discussed in Chapter 3, over many centuries men have learned to put women completely out of their lives, instead of having them as true helpmates through the complexities of life. Consequently, any valuable relationships or marriages that can be found are indeed exceptions. Because the old traditions have never been questioned, young men have not been trained in what to look for in life.

Man must clarify his principles. He must ask himself where he wants to put his creative seed. Seed is the creative power. Does he want his seed to produce something that is really worth producing? Jesus said some seeds fall on good soil, some on bad. Think: where do you want yours?

A man's identification cannot be with sex. He has to learn that nature's demand that he compete for females is not what his life is about. He must develop discrimination about sex and his choice of women. Not everything that is female should be good enough. That is animalistic. If a man would think of his self-worth, and know that his meditation or his prayer and his spiritual practices give his whole body a kind of different rhythm of vibration, then even if there is temptation, he would be able to discriminate about sex. A man's decision to be with a woman should not be made out of emotional need, sexual desire, a wish for domestic convenience, or a need to dominate. Principles about loyalty and marriage must be clarified before a relationship is undertaken.

The divine man, however, may not be so different from the divine woman. For thousands of years, much emphasis has been put on the difference between men and women. In many cultures there are very different rituals for boys and girls. This emphasis on differences may be leftovers from the animal kingdom. But human beings—male or female—have more in common than we like to think. We have grown up over the last few thousand years with denial of our similarities. This denial has to be eliminated.

Both men and women must reflect on the purpose of their lives and then work very hard to fulfill that purpose. The spiritual union that both must seek is the union with the Divine Power, which is neither male or female.

If men and women practice discrimination and restraint in procreation, there will be fewer opportunities for incarnations from selfish, greedy motives that result in inhumanity to others through wars, reprisals, and atrocities.

It is not important if the concept of reincarnation can be scientifically proven, but one thing we cannot deny is the course of our evolution. Each one, man or woman, has the power to direct that course in the most individual way, to steer the boat of his or her life through the stormy waters of destiny.

NOTES

[1]Gerder Lerner, *The Creation of Patriarchy* (New York: Oxford University Press, 1986). Lerner suggests that instead of searching for matriarchy, because it is so nebulous, it is better to search for the beginnings of patriarchy, to look at the beginnings of women's subordination, and the way they have contributed to it throughout history. *What has a beginning can have an end.*

Radha and Krishna's love—the Cosmic Play
has of course all the ingredients
of a love affair—spiritual and
erotic—aesthetic.

How else can an ordinary human
understand the Cosmic Play?
To be close will always be related
to best closeness experienced by
humans—

Lovers think of each other all the time.
In meditation every cell of being is on
the alert—like a lover expecting
the arrival of the Beloved.

The separation—the long waiting period.
This power of love is not to be
compared to wifely duties.

13 Seven Lives

THE PSYCHOLOGY OF YOGA provides the tools to achieve actual changes in thought, action, and consideration of others. For many centuries Yoga has been a practical science for improving the quality of life, but also for taking the individual practitioner far beyond the mundane level.

Most of the material for this book has emerged out of my thirty-five years in the practice and instruction of Yoga. During this time, many people have expressed their appreciation for the help they received, and described how effective the Teachings have been in improving their relationships and in transforming their personal lives.

For the purpose of illustration, I have chosen seven personal accounts of men and women who applied the principles in this book to their lives and in their relationships. Each story emphasizes a different aspect of the Teachings, showing how that person applied what had been learned. The people are real, though their names have been changed to protect their privacy. They have offered their accounts as practial examples of how the Teachings may be applied in daily life.

I hope this material will stimulate each reader to apply the concepts and ideas in this book to his or her own life.

MARY

Listening to people describe their experiences in family life, I have often wished they could have the opportunity of being under Swami Radha's guidance as I was. Marriage and family life became part of the process of spiritual life for me, rather than an end in themselves. I have often wanted to say to people, "There is much more. Don't stop there."

When I married, I was not "on the path." I was not reflecting on my life, or doing spiritual practices, or really taking responsibility for my emotions. I saw myself as a strong independent woman who often "struggled." These struggles frequently took me into weeks of depression that seemed to descend on me out of nowhere. In reality they were the accumulation of unresolved emotions that constantly had me on a teeter-totter. When Reid and I married in 1977 I was twenty-eight years old and had a daughter of four years. I felt that I was mature enough to be a good companion to Reid, and that we both could be a good parenting team for my daughter.

Reid and I quickly saw the Dream Lover in each other. This led to a very romantic start to the relationship that we felt was truly the "getting to know you" phase. When within the first year some real tests came our way, it was obvious that each of us had some problem areas to deal with, and we had no structure or support system to go to. This precipitated a depression in me, and I wondered if I had made a big mistake. Perhaps I wasn't cut out for marriage, perhaps I was *too* independent. Neither was the case. What in fact was happening was that my expectations were crumbling—unconsciously I had planned that this man would take care of me emotionally, and that of course we would live happily ever after. Expectations were high on both sides, and a basis of trust and friendship had not been built while we were being each other's Dream Lover.

Fortunately, the depression acted as a goad. A friend said to me, "Why don't you do something about the depression this time? You usually go away somewhere to make yourself feel better. How about getting some tools to help yourself?" I remember being miffed that my close friend would speak to me this way, but within a week I was on my way to Yasodhara Ashram to participate in a six-week course. This is when I stepped onto the path.

I started out complaining about my mate, how he didn't understand me and so on. I had many nightmares while there of our difficult interactions, but underneath it all I was sad that these barriers stood in our way. To find a means to go beyond the obstacles gave me great hope. Reflection, Mantra chanting, the Divine Light Invocation, and understanding the symbols of my dreams became my new support system. It became clear to me that I was projecting disappointments I had of myself onto Reid. It was *my* emotions that were out of control.

I returned home inspired to try a new approach, to change myself rather than Reid, and to begin spiritual practices. I did this, and the results were very encouraging. Long-term emotional patterns within myself did not disappear overnight. I had to really work at them over the next few years, but I eradicated the depression, which has never returned, and brought the tendencies that created them under conscious control.

Reid's response to the changes was first one of mistrust, but very quickly this turned to appreciation, and then a desire to explore the Teachings that were making such a difference for me. When we did a workshop together, he stepped onto the path.

What began to take place then, and continued over the next four years, was an increasing focus on the Divine. We still got into our trouble spots, and every few months there would be some kind of flare-up. But then I put Reid into the Light, or was able to say I was sorry, or we could chant together and take the interaction to another level.

In 1980 Reid and I did a Music and Consciousness workshop[1] with Swami Radha, and she told me I could not ignore the message I had given myself. I had an obligation to fulfill my potential over and above anything else. When Reid's pictures revealed the same path, and he got the same response from Swami Radha, it began to become clear that we each had the potential to reach Higher

Consciousness, and we could be a great help to each other.

A significant development did take place following this. We decided to become celibate. After taking the Yoga Development Course,[2] I had moved into a room of my own in our house. This was a bit odd for us both and felt like a separation initially, but it did not take long for the benefits of our own space to be obvious, and we settled into the change easily.

Our sexual life had been passionately romantic initially. As our difficulties emerged, we tended to use sex to make each other feel better, to make up, or to transform the intensity of our emotion with each other into some form of closeness. I was very needy and used sex in many ways to indulge my emotions. Looking back, I see that during the first years of marriage there was a selfishness in my sexual expression that tied in with wanting Reid to give me happiness.

In working with the Teachings, I realized that I could approach sexual contact in a very different way. I could put Reid first, put us both into the Light, and make intercourse something that sprang from a compassionate attitude rather than an indulgent one. This was a dry time. I remember trying to come from the heart, but feeling more as if I was fulfilling a duty. I knew I was on the right track, but Reid had lost some trust in me, and I had to work at what I was doing. During this time I had no interest in sex for myself.

Slowly, a new feeling began to grow between us. We had intercourse less frequently, but started making it a very special occasion. There was such an increase in quality and respect that we reflected this in intercourse. It was no longer indulgence or duty, but a very fine communication. We were beginning to grow up. Then on one of the weekend trips we regularly took to have some time together, neither of us felt like including intercourse in the evening. We talked for a long time, and very spontaneously decided to try a three-month period of celibacy. What is so important about this decision in retrospect for me is that morality had nothing to do with it. It just seemed like the next step. At the end of the three months neither of us felt we had a big decision to make. Celibacy made sense and we continued it.

Swami Radha said to me when I was struggling, "Keep your sights on the top of the mountain, rather than focusing so much on Reid. If both of you aim for the top and give each other enough space to climb up in your own way, in time your relationship will be very healthy." The analogy eluded me at the time, but I kept it alive in my mind over the years, and in fact this is what has transpired. This is what can happen for a married couple that focuses on the Teachings. For me it changed the definition of marriage.

Initially, my definition was unconscious. My parents' model was in my mind, and that, coupled with my expectations of Reid, formed the basis of it. I saw us as best friends, emotionally supporting each other, walking the path of life in harmony. We would be kind and loving parents. In fact, all this did happen, but it took some loosening up of concepts for me. Reid wasn't going to sit and hold my hand. He was extremely generous, but I was unable to appreciate this in him because I wanted him to express his generosity in my terms. But the more I let go, the more I could see the qualities in the human being I had married, and this was a wonderful discovery. I found such a very fine person under all those Dream Lover veils.

I found our definition of family life expanding over and over again. Swami Radha kept encouraging us to keep our focus on the spiritual.

We learned how to take a few minutes here or half an hour there, and really communicate with each other. So often I had heard Swami Radha say, "It is the quality of time together that is important, not the quantity." We did not take our time for granted, and the emotional barriers we had both been contending with began to dissolve.

There was a big shift in our relationship when I gained the courage to clarify and state where I saw us being able to support each other, and where I felt our emotional involvement pulling us down. In taking a stand on my reflections and following this up with action, I respected myself more, and Reid's respect for me increased. We emerged with a friendship and spiritual companionship that was characterized by deep acceptance and straightforward honesty. And we could really listen to each other. We started to bring out the best in each other.

We came face to face with our roles in the family, and it took some reflection and clarifying to accept that they were no longer valid.

My role as wife had to be expanded. My definition of nurturer and care-giver was very involved, and I had to let go of many of the aspects of this and take it to a higher level. I think that we were slowly stripping away the "becauses" in our love for each other. There has been a death of a certain kind of interaction for us, and yet we are both alive and healthy and moving toward the Light. This is a phase of marriage you don't often hear about.

On my part there was a level of possessiveness in my relationship with Reid that has dissolved in the last few years. I had not fully understood it.

Married life has so many levels to it: security (emotional and material), comfort, companionship, joint venture, coming face to face with yourself, learning to love and accept. That it can be lived in a very different way is evident by the couples who have lived under Swami Radha's guidance. It is a stepping-stone to Higher Consciousness if a focus on the Most High is given the rightful place within the union.

REID

Perhaps like many marriages, my own started from the basis of a deeply felt, emotionally charged idea of love. I was very much "in love," but as time would show, this was not the same as mature love, although it gave the impression of being so. I was to learn that being in love is not sufficient in itself to sustain such a major commitment. Mary and I were both idealistic people; in fact, this idealism was a strong binding force in our coming together. The difficulties arose for us in trying to bring the ideals that we both felt into line with the realities of two individuals attempting to make a life together. This presented us with a quandary that at one point threatened our marriage. On the one hand, the ideals that we shared were valuable and precious; on the other, personality, expectations, and a basic desire to have our needs met through each other undermined the ideals and began to create the pain of frustration and disappointment between us. Left unchecked this would have eventually destroyed the marriage.

Without knowing it, we were trying to fulfill a spiritual dimension in our lives through our marriage. What we didn't realize was that such a dimension can only be attained individually, through self-knowledge and personal responsibility. We found the way through the Teachings of Swami Radha's Yoga.

When I look at this now, I see how necessary it was for me to face facts. In spite of my feelings to the contrary, it was obvious that I did not understand much about love. Our first two years together had been heralded by an euphoric beginning followed by some pretty stormy, emotional times. This eventually led us to getting help, and that soon brought the Ashram and Yoga into our lives. Mary began with the six-week course in 1978, and in the fall of that year, an Ashram teacher came to our town to give us a Life Seal,[3] which was to be my first contact with the Ashram and the Teachings. Several workshops were to follow including a Music and Consciousness workshop with Swami Radha, which turned out to have particular significance for us. It became very apparent from that workshop that, from the perspective of consciousness, Mary and I were in a very similar place at the same time, and that there was much more at work here than the usual understanding of marriage. It was quite likely that we were, in the correct sense of the term, soul mates, and to a large degree our path together was already determined; we were here and together at this time to help each other on our spiritual journey, and for no other reason would we be together. I did not appreciate the full significance of this at the time, but our actions together following that Music and Consciousness workshop indicated that there was some understanding.

Yoga started the process by teaching us to stand back from each other in order to learn personal responsibility. In other words, to live emotional-mental independence, and thus begin to practice a different expression of love. I have come to understand marriage as the action field of the pairs of opposites, the creative dynamic of the mind. But obviously this action of creation has to be for a purpose or a specific direction other than for the continuance of an instinctual-emotional means of survival. I think I could only begin to see this with the gradual emotional detachment that came with a deepening understanding of Yoga and the path of awareness.

Swami Radha kindly took an interest in us and began to help us as much as she could. She would visit from time to time, and would always speak to the ideals that Mary and I were trying to live. Swami Radha would say, "Be considerate, even when you hold very different positions, and try to bring out the best in each other. If you speak to the Light in each other and not to the personalities, then the conflicts will end." And she was right in this. In time, this reinforcement of the Light in each other brought about a different way of seeing ourselves in marriage. In practical terms, the time came when I no longer identified myself as husband to Mary; in other words, my self-worth and purpose in life were not bound up with or dependent on my role in relation to her, and this was tremendously freeing for both of us. When this began to happen, I caught the first glimpses of the kind of love that Swami Radha talked about: love without attachment, love that is able to give freely without the object of getting in return. In realistic terms, this did not just fall upon us from out of the heavens. This understanding resulted from working with the Teachings of Yoga: doing the Light Invocation together, doing a Mantra practice that helped me learn the art of emotional control, and recognizing that through the spiritual practices of Yoga we were bringing the quality into our marriage that we had so desired from the beginning.

The other key step for us was to learn, through the work in Kundalini Yoga, to question our purpose in marriage, to examine what was our understanding of sex and what were our expectations of each other, and why, if we accepted the idea of a divine power in our lives, would such a power have brought us together in the first place? Important questions, and not ones that I would have normally thought to ask. And also very challenging questions that required some confidence and courage to ask. But they emerged out of a body of teaching that I had begun to trust, because the work that we had done in Yoga had, without question, improved the quality of our marriage immeasurably. As Swami Radha often said, "Your experience will be the best measure for you of whether or not the Teachings can work for you. It is not in what I say, but in your experience, and *that* you can trust." Perhaps the most telling experience came about two or three years after we had begun our work in Yoga, over the issue of sex in our marriage. This is what happened:

Now and again, we would go away for a weekend, just the two of us. We would stay in a nice place, have a really good dinner, a special treat, and we would have a special sexual intimacy, too. Now it happened on one of these weekends that Mary asked me, in our room after dinner, what did I really think about sex? Or she asked something like that. Anyway, the conversation that followed seemed to come from a deep and spontaneous place in each of us, simultaneously. We really didn't want to have sex; somehow it wasn't important enough to make a big deal over. And I remember this realization as coming to us in the most gentle and loving language, coming from a deep place within each of us. From that night on, we were celibate and have remained so, as naturally as could be. We were now free to acknowledge the deep friendship that was also a fundamental building block for our marriage. That friendship, without the manipulative dynamic of sex, remains most precious to me.

Christine

My marriage took place in the mid-forties at a time when women were under the influence of strong cultural and social pressures, including the impact of wars in Europe and the South Pacific. The first influence created the assumption that marriage was the expected direction for women to pursue, and family life was something in which fulfillment was expected to occur. The influence of war psychology created an urgency to grab some happiness now, as the future was completely uncertain with men entering the armed services and embarking for overseas.

I was influenced as well by a secure childhood with loving parents who had a solid marriage. I wanted to duplicate this situation, and the insecurity of the political scene reinforced the urgency to do it now. In spite of the fact that I attended a top women's college and was exposed to other options, the conditioning was too strong. I did consider serving the country by joining the WAVES, the women's branch of the Navy, but the pull of the relationship I was involved in was too powerful. I see now how young and inexperienced we were. We resisted the urging of my parents to wait. I ended up cutting short my college years in order to get married, and to follow my husband to the Army Air Force camp where he was stationed until he was sent overseas.

I became pregnant before he left, and the direction of my life was set. Little thought was given to the future impact of our actions, although I was aware of that strong instinctual emotional desire to have babies. I have not regretted this part of my life, because once I took on that responsibility of raising my children, I found it rewarding and quite a learning experience. Yet that had to be the focus of my life for the next fifteen years. No compromise, no giving up, even when the marriage went through some very rocky times.

As my spiritual search began to grow in importance, I realized that my husband and I were growing into individuals very different from the ones we were when we made those idealistic marriage vows to "love, honor, and obey till death do us part." Who made those vows? A part of me that clung to the belief that somehow everything would work out, that marriage was wonderful and beautiful. Wasn't that evident in my parents' marriage? I was in love with the idea of love, and the perfect marriage, and the Dream Lover. But my husband was not that Dream Lover, and both of us were growing and changing in many ways that did not fit that ideal picture. I kept trying to make us fit into a picture, but it didn't work.

Gradually I became aware of the inspiration and balance provided by a spiritual influence moving into focus in my life. When this longing urged me to *do* something, I sent out a prayer for help, because I did not have anyone to guide me toward a way of bringing a concrete expression of a spiritual way of being into my life. Within a few months I received an invitation to join an Edgar Cayce Search for God group in my area, and I was on my way.

My husband did not object to my activities, but at the same time he showed no interest. At first I tried to explain to him what I was doing, hoping he would join me, but I came to see that this was not fair. He had his own interests and hobbies, which took up his free time.

More and more I found myself divided, my life split between my growing involvement with my inner search, with the new friends developing from this, and the outer pull of married life with its responsibilities and social obligations.

I can see now that the choices I made were symbolic of the direction my life was taking, and the growing commitment to my spiritual growth. I kept wondering how I could continue to carry on with the marriage, and still develop my spiritual potential. As a further test for me, my husband was involved in another relationship. How could I live with someone I no longer trusted? Was I expecting too much of my marriage of twenty-five years? Was this a test to apply spiritual principles in a difficult situation? My energy was continually drawn to these issues that pulled me in so many directions. I spent a lot of time looking at options and trying to find solutions to the problems. Pride prevented me from seeking help. No one in my family had ever been separated or divorced. How could I do such a thing and bring shame on the family?

Looking back with a different perspective, I wonder if the tests and difficulties were the means of strengthening my commitment even more to my spiritual growth. I had to clarify my own values and spiritual principles. I had to decide what I really wanted to do with my life.

It was going to the Ashram that opened up a new world to me and gave me the tools I needed to clarify. Swami Radha gave firm, clear guidance and support, but always with quiet patience and compassion. I had to make my own decisions and take responsibility for them. But in this process there was a growing sense of relief mixed with the anxiety of an uncertain future.

The difficulty my husband and I had communicating was faced head on as I presented my suggestion that we each write a paper on how we felt about our marriage and what our options were. This set into motion a process of clarification and communication. The outcome was an agreement to separate for a while, to give each other space and time to think about the next step. Now I see the importance of keeping open the lines of communication, which we had not been able to do over the years.

I also see how the Teachings I learned and absorbed from Swami Radha gave me increasing courage and stability to take the action that needed to be taken to put the Divine first in my life. Although there was pain in breaking up a relationship of so many years, I found it didn't have to be done with ill feeling or resentment. I used the tools I had been given to work through the separation and the conflicting feelings that surfaced.

It was my choice to move out of the house we had built together and filled with memories of twenty-five years of living together. I needed my own space to allow the new person I was becoming to expand and grow. I think this was a vital part of my sense of freedom. I set up a prayer room for my practice, and I had an empty room for Hatha Yoga classes, something I never could have done in the house I shared with my husband. It took a year of sorting through feelings and coming to terms with my past before I was able to move into the next phase of my life. I still had to deal with the sense of separation and a splitting off of part of myself.

It was a number of years after our separation that we decided on a divorce. It was important to wait until the time was right for us. When we finally got a divorce, I had a ceremony to conclude the final chapter of that part of my life. It was creating an ending without resentment or regrets.

I could spend a lot of time reflecting on "What if I had not gotten married when I was so young?" "What if I had not waited so long to . . . ?" and so on. There are many "what if's." But I see nothing to be gained in doing this. There are more important questions to be answered: What have I learned from my experiences? How can I use that learning now? What am I doing with my life? What do I want to do with my life in the future? What *is* the purpose of my life? I honor the good that was in my past; I do not want to throw out the good parts as I discard what was not constructive. I feel as if I have the freedom now to fulfill my own evolution as a spiritual being. I have taken major steps in this direction.

SARAH

The story of my marriage is the story of letting go of dependency.

Being a happily married woman on the yogic path has been a tremendous support, and a tremendous challenge. I've come to see that it is not easier or harder for one to be married—just different.

When I came to the yogic path I was twenty-four years old, and newly married—less than a year. I was very "happy." I had a great respect and affection for my husband, Malcolm, and we cared deeply for each other. I had an exciting job, good health, good friends, financial security, talent and ability—all of the things most people strive for, especially A Good Relationship: isn't that supposed to be "it"? It startled me to discover, after only a few months of marriage, that it *wasn't* "it." That all the support and affection and understanding wasn't enough. Something was missing.

I can see now that here is where a happy marriage can be such an advantage on the path—because once you have that much-sought-after prize, you also have the opportunity to realize it isn't enough. If you haven't had that experience, you may spend your life striving to find it.

And so I found myself looking around me for help—help to even figure out what was wrong. I tried some sessions with a psychiatrist. The fact that these sessions didn't help was in itself helpful, because it made me realize that what was "wrong" was that I was beginning to wake up to the sense that life had a deeper meaning than just comfort, support, and intimacy. I had been asking the question for some time, although not consciously, What is the purpose of my life?

I had been writing down my dreams for some months. I didn't know what to do with them. I decided that perhaps a Jungian therapist (since they work with dreams) might be my key. In seeking out such a therapist, I asked another psychiatrist friend for advice. To his great credit, he perceived what I was really at basis seeking, and recommended that I instead talk with his wife who was involved in Yoga. I did so, and she suggested that I take a workshop with her Guru, Swami Radha.

Meeting with Swami Radha awoke something deep within me, and everything began to "move" in me toward the Divine.

I returned for a few more workshops, and I saw that the reason Swami Radha and her teachers could help others was that they knew, from their own experience of using the tools in their own lives, what worked. They lived what they spoke. I wanted to learn what they knew, and to help others from the level of personal experience as they did.

My husband was quite dubious, and basically didn't want to talk too much about what I was becoming involved in. We had shared so much up to this point—would the spiritual come between us? I began to push, to try to nudge or coerce or argue him into taking an interest. This backfired, and he retreated even more. Three months into it, I again woke up and realized what I was doing. I was trying to impose on him my view of what he should be, of what being "spiritual" meant. By what right did I think I could try to change him? I realized that, at basis, to be spiritual meant to lead a life of integrity, and this he was doing. So I very deliberately gave up my desire for him to change, and replaced it with appreciation for his spiritual nature. Every day I "gave him to God" in prayer, asking the Divine to keep him in the Light, consciously letting go of my expectations and desires. This freed us both. I stopped being afraid of the future, and carried on with my own spiritual quest.

So I went across the country to the Yoga Development Course at Yasodhara Ashram, leaving my husband and my job behind for three months.

The Yoga Development Course: ninety days of full-time intensive soul-searching. I sent Malcolm a tape recording of a two-hour session I had early in the YDC—a Life Seal workshop. Being involved in mental health work as a counselor himself, he had been deeply impressed with the "therapy" that had been done with me. So impressed, that he said he would like to learn to do the same thing!

I could hardly believe my ears, and said to him that he didn't need to say that for my benefit. But he was adamant. He came to visit me for five days during the course, and was allowed to sit in on workshops. At the end of the five days he had decided to return the following year to take the Course himself!

It would be easy to conclude, from what happened to me, that if one surrenders the marriage relationship to the Divine, the partner "comes around" to following the spiritual path. I don't think that's necessarily the case. But I do know that if I had *not* surrendered the relationship, I would have bulldozed Malcolm so far off the Path that he likely wouldn't ever have gone anywhere near it.

Swami Radha suggested that I return the following year, if possible, and do the Yoga Development Course with him. We both quit our jobs and came. Doing the course with Malcolm was a very different experience: it was much more challenging. I discovered that the aspect of my life about which I felt the most protective was my marriage. Because that was where my security lay. I realized that I had been nurturing the illusion that we had The Perfect Marriage. The illusion was dispelled in the YDC, and this was quite frightening for me. I felt disoriented, upside-down, confused. As Malcolm began to change in all the ways I had hoped he might, I got even more upset. Nothing was the same, everything was changing. What was happening to my secure, predictable world? He seemed like a stranger, and I wasn't even sure he was a stranger I would like!

But gradually I regained equilibrium and began to appreciate the changes. I began to appreciate what it means to be on the spiritual path as a couple. It has meant that we try to support the very best part of each other—the part that wants to know the Divine, that wants to put the Divine first. If one of us got discouraged or stuck, the other would often help him or her to get back on track. We sometimes did practices together, which was a good support. Malcolm was as enthusiastic as I, and Yoga quickly became the priority in both of our lives.

But our commitment to the path had not yet been tested. It was still the honeymoon period. I think we needed that period for the Divine to become so established in our hearts that we could meet the challenges when they came.

It was during this early time that we began to explore options in our sexual relationship. As I became more involved in Yoga, areas of unclear thinking, or matters of conscience, became harder to ignore. One day I realized that I was unwilling to risk an unwanted pregnancy, and that any form of birth control other than the Pill left me open to this possibility. For health reasons I couldn't take the Pill, so had been using more risky methods.

Swami Radha offered to work with us on the issue of our sexual relationship, and we gratefully accepted her help. She had us write about what we thought sex was, what our concepts were about it, and what were our preferences. As the process of sending tapes and letters back and forth to her unfolded, I realized that she did not at all think sex was wrong or bad, as I had assumed she would. She didn't suggest celibacy—in fact, she warned us that it was difficult to be a celibate for more than two years, unless one really felt drawn to it. And if, she said, all the extra energy provided by being celibate is used in the struggle to *be* celibate, then what's the point?

Neither of us was seriously considering celibacy, but we were interested in oral sex as a possible solution to my dilemma. She discouraged that idea because, she said, it is difficult to be satisfied with only oral sex. Tubal ligation was a possibility she suggested that we explore—that being preferable to vasectomy, given that Malcolm still wanted children and I did not. If he should ever remarry, he would then have the option to have them. Swami Radha also suggested we work with a sexual practice called *karezza* as described in von Urban's book, *Sex Perfection*. In this practice, there is no genital contact at all, but sexual energy can potentially be redirected to a higher level.

We began to work with this practice. Gradually, over the space of several months, we found a peculiar thing happening: we both found ourselves becoming drawn to being celibate. This is hard to explain, as there was certainly no diminishing in our level of caring for each other.

I certainly was not becoming celibate to please Swami Radha. In fact, I felt for a long time that I had let her down, that she had been keen to have us try this karezza method, and I had failed to achieve what it was designed to do. Years later, she laughed when I told her this story, and said, "You succeeded beyond my hopes!"

I suppose I may have unconsciously seen celibacy as the easiest way out of a sexual dilemma, although it didn't seem like that at the time, nor does it now. Swami Radha also later challenged me to consider whether one reason I didn't want to have children was my self-ishness. I suspect there is some reality to that. But I don't think it's the main factor. I think I knew somewhere deep inside that I wanted to give my all to the Divine.

As Malcolm moved along the path, his dedication to it grew until he finally realized he truly didn't want to have children because he wanted to put his energy into the path. I think he may also have become less romantic about what having children means. It was around that time that a friend visited with her hyperactive two-year-old son!

One day Malcolm told me he would like to have his own room rather than share one with me. Particularly, he wanted to have his own bed, as he said he found my emotions too much to "rub elbows with" at night. He didn't say this critically—just as a fact. I was briefly hurt and threatened, but adjusted to living in separate rooms quite well. I see this now as another concrete step in becoming less dependent and "enmeshed."

Although having sex had never been a strong desire on my part, physical affection *had* been. In fact, it had been as big a bone of contention between us as had been the issue of how frequently to have intercourse: I often wanted more hugs, and he often wanted more intercourse—a very common difference between men and women, I've since discovered. So giving up the physical affection of sharing the same bed was difficult for me. But then we soon learned that one can't be celibate and still have much touching anyway (at least not at first).

The challenge for Malcolm and me has never been to "get along," as it is for so many couples. The challenge has been to let go. It's been hard for us to put the Divine first, before the relationship.

A few years later I went through a period of depression. I now see that it was essential to begin to bring me out of dependency. It made things so bad that I had to go much further than just doing the right things on the surface: I had to change. It was a shock to discover that Malcolm couldn't help me. I had to experience that aloneness that is the reality of life, before I could begin to let go.

This process of letting go of dependency would take six more years before it would fully bear fruit—which again speaks for the hold it has had on me. But I did begin to let go during the depression. How did I do that? I stopped doing things to please others. I looked within for answers to what I needed. But the depression didn't teach me all I needed to know. It got me out of being a little girl and into being an adolescent: an improvement, but only that. I still clung to Malcolm.

He began to travel and be away a lot of the time, so I couldn't turn to him whenever I wanted support or someone to listen to me talk, and so I began to notice how dependent I still was on him, in these ways. This period of intermittent separation lasted two years. I developed more self-reliance during that time.

It was during this time that we received Mantra initiation from Swami Radha. Obedience is important in the Guru-disciple relationship, and before initiation I began to be concerned about what obedience might mean in terms of Malcolm's and my relationship.

I was also going through major basic questioning regarding my future. I drew a Life Map,[4] which ended in a choice of directions and a big question mark. The doubts and fears, all centering on dependency, had been building and building until they broke out in this one big question: Did I want to continue on this Path? At the time, I wouldn't have phrased it so boldly, but now I see it so.

Then one day, during some chanting, I had an experience: I suddenly wanted to give Malcolm to the Divine. The urge came with a tremendous feeling of trust and joy, and it set something in motion within me. Sometime later I knew, in a flash, that I wanted, more than anything, to go as far as I could go on the path. The relief of really knowing was tremendous, and catapulted me into a high state for weeks. I found myself eager to do intensive practice every day, in a way and to a depth I had never experienced before. Something within me had got settled, got resolved and decided. I found out that

I knew—had known all along—what is most important to me.

I see that many of us couples on the path now are coming to a similar conclusion—that we need more independence from our mates in order to go further. And now I find myself encouraging others.

MALCOLM

My wife and I both felt we had a particularly good marriage. It wasn't that there was anything wrong, but something seemed to be missing that I couldn't put my finger on. I could foresee what lay ahead—buying a house, rising in the work that we did, perhaps having parents come to live with us when they grew older. The prospects were all good, but something was still incomplete.

Change began when Sarah decided she would like to spend a couple of weeks in intensive therapy with a psychiatrist who came to our plant as a consultant. Perhaps he would have some questions to ask that could help reveal what the issue was. We had both worked with Mark, and we knew that he was good, but when Sarah was with him in those two weeks as a patient, there was something missing in their sessions, too. Finally Mark said, "There's an area we psychiatrists are comfortable working in, and we're good at it, but when we come close to what's considered to be spiritual, that's beyond our line of work. That seems to be where you want to go, and I can't go with you there. It's possible a Jungian therapist would help."

Now Sarah was being told that psychiatry couldn't help her find the answers she was looking for, because where she was looking was traditionally the bailiwick of religion. And I had given up religion. So Sarah was headed out on her own.

The wife of another psychiatrist we knew well was a Yoga teacher, and she offered to teach introductory classes in our community during the week that her husband was consulting with the plant.

Things quickly moved on from there. This was what Sarah was after. In short order she took several workshops with Swami Radha, and decided to take the three-month Yoga Development Course at the Ashram.

Not long after the course began, while we were talking on the phone Sarah mentioned that she had taken a workshop called Life Seal, that it had been good, and that she had taped it. I was curious to find what was happening to her, so I asked if she would send me the tape. A request like that from a husband with no interest in Yoga, was more than Sarah dreamed of. And once I had heard the tape I called Sarah and said, "The quality of work that was done in the Life Seal was finer than any work I've seen anyone do."

Sarah suggested that when I came to the Ashram I could meet the man who had worked with her, a man her age who was a swami, and who had learned everything he did from the lady who had founded the Ashram. And *she* had been a German dancer who at forty-five had spent six months in India with her teacher, and he had transformed her life.

During the week that I was there, the students did a simple exercise in class called "Who are you?" Later Sarah and I decided we would like a day to ourselves, so we took the ferry across the lake to the hot springs, and spent the night there. And during that evening, we did the exercise together.

Again I couldn't put the experience well into words, but I realized that in this time of asking and answering, this was the most intimate experience I had had with Sarah. Until then I had thought that emotional intimacy was directly connected with physical intimacy, and here I discovered that the two weren't necessarily correlated at all. I had gone somewhere within Sarah, and she in me, that we had never gone into as deeply before. And we had been sitting in chairs asking a simple question again and again. What was at work?

When Sarah returned from the Development Course, she was wise enough to say little about what happened, and to answer only what I asked. So I felt myself under no pressure to be involved in what had come to mean so much to her. She had brought back tapes of chanting, and played them sometimes while she cooked or ironed, and I found them particularly bothersome: it was the same phrase chanted repeatedly by an untrained voice, and I found it grating. That took some negotiating to resolve, because the chanting helped keep

Sarah focused upon what she was doing and why she was doing it. But because I found the tapes so unattractive, she chose to play them only when she was alone.

The Yoga Development Course had pointed Sarah clearly in the direction she wanted to go, but she had taken the course alone. Since I would be taking the course in the following year, and because Sarah knew that taking the YDC with her mate would be a very different experience, she decided to join me and take it a second time.

There was enough of the hippie left in me that I came to the Ashram with beard and long hair. And I wore glasses, so there wasn't much of me that wasn't covered with something. Midway in the course we were asked to write a paper on the perfect marriage, and while we talked about our papers, I said something about openness and expressiveness. If that was a goal in my marriage, I was throwing up several obstacles to it simply by masking myself with hair and glass. Well, *that* was something I could change *now*, and I did. Within an hour I had taken off the beard I had worn for seven or eight years, and a resident volunteered as a barber, and now my hair was short as well.

This was a step Sarah had been wanting for a long time, but now the reality was particularly unpleasant. Sarah found my face almost repugnant, and she found it difficult sharing a room with me. Physically I was a new man to her.

I had always had a particular affinity for children, especially young ones. I seemed to attract them like a magnet, and now admit with some chagrin that I often preferred their company to the company of adults. I had always assumed I would be a father. It was one of those natural progressions—one gets married and has children. At the outset Sarah had said she enjoyed the company of children, but had no desire to be a mother. But I thought that would be something that could be fixed in time. She would come around.

In the "Perfect Marriage" paper, I had written as best I could why I wanted to be a father. Was it pure self-gratification to want little replicas of Sarah and me running around the house? Then perhaps that was only instinct at work, wanting to replicate my genes. If it truly was wanting to help new life, why not truly help by fostering or adopting? Did the world need one more bundle of karma that I selfishly wanted to create? And if I truly wanted to provide the atmosphere for a soul to return, and be nourished in a home that valued these things, was that adequate motivation? I worked on it over and over in my head. Sarah and I had talked about it many times. But no resolution. So I took the issue to my dreams. I went to bed with the question in my mind, "What is truly best for me? Should I become a father?" And for six weeks I had not one dream. Not one. So part of me was asking the questions, and another part wasn't ready for the answer.

At the end of the summer we returned home, but kept contact with Swami Radha. Often I found these conversations with her quite disorienting. Part of the disorientation was the result of being shown so many possibilities, but the major part was simply being put and kept in the Light the whole time we talked.

During one such call, Swami Radha asked, "How much longer do you want to remain a seeder, Malcolm? Do you think it's possible to move beyond instinct and the dictates of your genes? What freedom might there be in such a move?" The word *seeder* was so primitive and limiting. But she asked in such a way that it was impossible to take offense. She also aroused my curiosity.

And in later conversations we talked extensively about how we might continue expanding what it meant to live a spiritual life, and have a spiritual marriage.

We found that visualizing the Light before and during intercourse elevated those moments into something quite rare. And although Swami Radha was a sanyasin and a celibate, she was able to suggest how any experience could be refined. During the YDC we had read extracts from von Urban's book in which he taught karezza, and now Swami Radha reminded us of it. Would we like to explore those possibilities? And in another conversation she talked about Tantra Yoga, and said that Yoga is a path of many paths. From the many, you choose the one that appeals most. Which you choose is almost irrelevant, just as driving by Volkswagen, Chevrolet, or Peugeot doesn't really matter, because each can get you where you want to go.

Sarah came to realize that any method of contraception asked too much—none was certain, and many had unhealthy side-effects. We continued our sexual relationship, but now it didn't involve penetration.

And the changes continued over time. I felt an increasing need to have a place of my own. After Sarah and I had had a disagreement, even if we had made up afterward, I still found it difficult sleeping in the same bed, with the remnants of that atmosphere still in the air. So one day I decided that I would be moving into the next room. Now we would be together by choice rather than necessity or habit. That was a hard one for Sarah to understand, for her to see it as anything but rejection. Because I was doing the initiating, because I was doing the moving, her reaction took me by surprise. That seems often to be the case in a relationship: the one who changes sees what's ahead as a natural and attractive progression, while the other partner feels he or she is being "done to," rejected, or left behind. I didn't understand her reaction, until later when the roles were reversed. *Then* I understood, because then I was on the receiving end, and reacting the same way.

In the several conversations that we had with Swami Radha, soon the subject of spiritual practice came up. "Your relationship with the Divine is as intimate as a love affair. Your conversations are secret. What happens when the two of you are together could not really be described to anyone else, even if you wanted to, so don't even attempt to describe it."

Sarah and I had been accustomed to being very free in talking with each other. Talking was a means to intimacy. And now Swami Radha was saying that here was one aspect of our daily lives we weren't to discuss. That went against our way of being together. But at least we would try it. I found myself wondering how Sarah was doing. Was she getting up at a certain hour, and how long was her practice? Then I realized that Sarah didn't know what was happening for me, either, whether it was hard slogging or effortless. And *then* some weight was taken off my shoulders. No one knew what I was doing in this time, and so I could be free. Comparison and competition had been removed. Another rule about marriage had been broken. And we both had more freedom.

As time went on, Sarah began feeling increasingly desperate, and didn't know where to turn. One night she woke me, asked if I could come to her bed and hold her. And I held on tight. But no matter how close or tight I held her, I couldn't help. That was a watershed. No matter how strong my desire to help, no matter how strong her desire to be helped, there were things that I simply couldn't do for her.

So what was happening to our marriage? The proof was in the result of what we did, not in the trappings of what a marriage should be. We became less entangled with each other, and came closer to each other.

At one time I said to Swami Radha, "My understanding is that you find no fault with marriage, but that in order to become fully independent and free, one must leave marriage behind, no matter how good it is."

And she said, "Yes. You remember that Ma-chig-lag, the Tibetan, talked about demons and dragons, that it is often what you profess to love the most that holds you back." Swami Radha was clear that at some point marriage has to be left behind, so that my spiritual pursuit is total and without distraction. But where was I with this?

First I looked closely at what our marriage was based on. During our wedding ceremony we had said we would be together for a long time. We couldn't say "forever," because we wanted to say only what we knew was true. It was an unpleasant prospect, but perhaps something would draw one of us away from the other, and we had to acknowledge that at the outset, rather than make promises we couldn't keep with certainty. And we had said we would attempt to draw out the best in each other.

Cultivating the best in each other was still the foundation of our relationship. Our increasing independence from each other, longer time apart, were making each of us people in our own right, distinct from Sarah-and-Malcolm, and Malcolm-and-Sarah. Was that my goal—total independence—so that it didn't matter whether or not I saw Sarah? How dependent was I, and how independent and distinct did I want to become?

How to truly know? That was the question that stayed with me: How to know? Swami Radha was emphatic on her position: what people call love is only gonads at work. It's all a mating dance she would say, over and over. There is no such thing as love, she said, because it all came back to some level of gratification: I say I "love" because I receive some benefit or reward from the person I profess to love. Once the reward disappears, so does the love.

My relationship with Sarah had always been of great importance in my life, if not the most important thing in my life. I cared for her profoundly. My caring for her had little or nothing to do with gonads because we had been celibate now for years. Then what reward was there in the relationship for me, and was the reward wrong? Did I depend upon the reward? And was my dependence upon it, or attachment to it, detracting me from my goal of an intimate connection with the Divine?

I found I could distill the questions down to one: are marriage and my pursuit of the Divine mutually exclusive?

Swami Radha saw marriage itself as no obstacle whatever. It was the possession and dependence binding partners to each other that was the obstacle. In her view, if I could become more independent within the marriage, if I could release my mate from my emotional possessiveness, then Swami Radha had no objection to marriage at all. Then my mate and I could pursue the spiritual path together, each in our own way. Our ways and times of practice might be different: perhaps one preferred morning and the other preferred evening for reflection, or each used a different Mantra. If that freedom could be found in marriage, then she would support it.

I had read and listened, and I had taken spirituality as far as logical mind could take me. I knew what I "should" do. And over time I realized that if I did what I should, there would be no life in it for me. Spiritual life is to be embraced, not to be borne like a cross. "Given where I am now, given my present understanding, given what draws me, how can I live a spiritual life?" Once I phrased the question *that* way, I knew what my answer was.

So what now to do with these two perceptions: one believing that a close relationship inhibited a close connection with the Divine, and the other believing that it was a *route* to the Divine? Both of us felt sad because on one level this was as far apart as we had ever been, and both of us had a part in us that wished the other saw things differently. And most important, despite the sadness, we realized that we must each go another step in letting the other go, because that's what we had promised at the beginning: that we would attempt to bring out the best in each other. We hoped but could not promise that we would be together forever. Our time together has been most remarkable—most clearly a profound divine gift.

Who knows what is yet to come?

Jane

When I step back and ask myself: How have Swami Radha's Teachings influenced my life? three key areas come to mind. The first is a quest for honesty and an effort to live my everyday life with an integrity that comes from what I have learned and now *know*. The second is the ongoing lesson of increasing my ability to be respectful and considerate of others. And finally, the Teachings and the process that Swami Radha encourages is helping me learn greater and greater self-reliance.

Expanding the question to ask how her Teachings have influenced Robert's and my relationship, I would answer in the same way: the Teachings have encouraged us

1. to seek honesty with each other
2. to be considerate of one another
3. to move toward greater self-reliance

The greatest blessing of this relationship for me is that we met, and the relationship took its initial form while we were both in the intensive Yoga Development Course at the Ashram. For three months, day after day, we wrote papers and read them aloud in a group setting, and in that process, got to know each other in a much more real way than what usually happens when two people meet and begin to get to know each other. Although we certainly continue to deal with our fantasies and illusions about love and each other, there was less room for them at the beginning of our relationship because of the process we were in. We also abstained sexually for the first several months, and I think this strengthened the relationship tremendously. Sex can throw a veil over the facts of what is, and can immediately and very powerfully introduce expectations, possessiveness, and the stickiness of dependency. The simplest way I can say it is that we got to know each other as friends, as two people—not a couple—first.

The process of self-exploration continued for us, following the Ashram stay. For three years, we lived a thousand miles apart (seeing each other briefly every three months), but continued to write papers for clarification under the guidance of one of the Ashram teachers. Once a year we would return to the Ashram, and that stay always included a private session focused on the relationship.

Then two years ago, I moved to the city where Robert lived—we were ready to experiment with living together. Because of my own patterns of dependency, though, I wanted a time of transition to strengthen my own awareness and independence. The choice was made to go to the Ashram for two and a half months to live and work before we actually began living together.

Our first year under the same roof had many of the same ups and downs that most couples experience: facing expectations and fears, trying to change the other, focusing too much on the other person, struggling with issues of possessiveness. One of the very best decisions we made was to follow up on one of Swami Radha's suggestions to have separate bedrooms. This allows for a greater sense of independence and privacy, and a kind of newness or freshness whenever we do sleep in the same room.

Robert and I met in the Light of Swami Radha's Teachings, and it *is* the Teachings that give us a way of working through difficulties, of celebrating victories, of seeing our relationship in a proper perspective: as a vehicle for now, in helping us both live more closely our life purposes. We find ways of continually reminding ourselves that the purpose of our relationship is to help us grow—doing the Divine Light Invocation together, returning to the Ashram when we can, continuing to write papers and read them to each other, learning to be more honest and open in our communication with each other. The Teachings have been the "glue" of our relationship, as Robert recently said, and the rewards of our growing awareness and learning are immense.

ROBERT

The influence that Swami Radha and her Teachings have had on my relationship with Jane can be expressed by words such as quality and integrity, deeper connection, struggle to understand and breaking through fears. There is, however, one quality that the Teachings have brought to me and our relationship, that stands out above the rest, and that is the ability to be constantly questioning my actions, fears, and desires around the relationship.

Questioning in a relationship is a powerful practice. It means our relationship is alive and evolving. Personally it prevents me from being distant and at times indifferent. The communication that takes place between Jane and me through the questions we ask, or that Swami Radha asks us, enables me to dissolve some of the illusions I hold about relationships, and in doing so continually tests the quality of our relationship.

I am also grateful for the Teachings, because without them I might never have asked the important questions, which range from the most profound (Why have Jane and I come together in this relationship, and what is its purpose?) to the more practical questions that deal with the role of sex, ways to show consideration, etc. One of the more pragmatic questions that the Teachings brought to the relationship was whether we should have separate bedrooms. While the answer came quickly (in the affirmative), I'm not sure I would have ever asked the question if I had not been introduced to the Teachings of Swami Radha. Questioning has therefore provided realistic and creative options to our relationship.

Questions require answers to be then followed by action. The Teachings again provide insight, facts, and wisdom that help me discover the answers within myself. The various workshops that I have attended have taught me the value and reliability of such tools (or practices) as Mantra and visualization, reflection papers, and dream interpretations in providing answers to even the most complex questions. These tools have become trusty companions in resolving questions, and even after six years I am still amazed at how reliable they can be in providing clear, relevant, timely, and appropriate answers.

Perhaps the greatest gift from Swami Radha's work has been the faith and security of knowing that the Teachings do provide a constant source of understanding, and this inevitably leads to answers. This then provides me with a freedom to further explore and question my relationship with Jane. They are wonderfully supportive in this way—which is not to say that I always find the answers easy to accept, but then I go back to my trust in the practices, and realize that if I have been honest, then the answer is what I need to know.

Finally, the knowledge that the Teachings are directly connected with an ancient and profound wisdom and to Divine Mother is personally very liberating. It encourages me to work diligently and openly within our relationship.

I asked Swami Radha, one evening, "What happens to couples who don't have access to the profound and essential questions?"

She immediately replied, "They have problems!"

While our relationship is not without problems (or issues, as I prefer to call them) the questions that Swami Radha has asked us to look at, whether directly, or through the workshops, or through her book *Kundalini Yoga for the West,* have continually moved our relationship forward. In fact, I am convinced if we stopped asking the important questions and did not have access to the wisdom of the Teachings, our relationship might wither into a mechanical, lifeless pattern of responding to expectations and social convention.

I would be remiss if I did not mention that our relationship began as friends at the Ashram, the spiritual community that embodies Swami Radha's Teachings. But meeting at the Ashram provides no assurance of developing a committed and evolving relationship. However, the application of the Teachings, learned at the Ashram, has been crucial to the purpose of our relationship. The added opportunity of being able to write papers together and send them to the Ashram, observe couples at the Ashram and, most importantly, meet with one of the long-term residents, has been essential in helping me to break out of the illusions of traditional relationships. The awareness of the Divine and trusting Her knowledge has been introduced to me through the Teachings, and they have become the strength of our relationship.

NOTES

[1]"Music and Consciousness" is an Ashram workshop in which participants draw symbols.

[2]The Yoga Development Course is an intensive three-month personal development course given at Yasodhara Ashram.

[3]"Life Seal" is an Ashram workshop in which participants draw symbols that allow unconscious messages to emerge.

[4]"Life Map" is an Ashram workshop, now called "Pathways."

Some souls are attracted
by glittering luxuries,
allowing indulgences,
great passion, selfishness
nourished by pride.
Exaggerated ego demanding
satisfaction at any cost:
blood flows, heads roll,
hearts torn apart. Hunger
and pain are rewards of all
slanderers of compassion.

Returning to the grave gives
no new promise of
paradise. What then?
Where is the purpose of it all—
life after life—if no
purpose is recognized?
Miracle of grace
lightens the blackness that
covered the mind.
Light, some light, any light
would be a blessing for the
killer and the survivor.

Light of consciousness,
Divine Light, illumination,
a way to Liberation.

Hard-won freedom,
vibration of heavenly sound,
fire of compassion regenerated.
Light-filled mind and heart.
What better purpose than
to be a bodhisattva?

Bibliography

Adams, Margaret. *Single Blessedness: Observations on the Single Status in Married Society.* New York: Basic Books, Inc., 1976. Adams has written a "generous and unapologetic celebration of unmarried life in a married society."

Allione, Tsultrim. *Women of Wisdom.* London: Routledge & Kegal Paul, 1984. This book is an exploration and celebration of the spiritual potential of all women, as exemplified by the lives of six great Tibetan women. There have been few stories of women who have achieved illumination, and therefore few models for women to emulate.

Anderson, Bonnie S., and Judith P. Zinsser. *A History of Their Own: Women in Europe from Prehistory to the Present.* New York: Harper & Row, 1989. A ground-breaking and controversial history of European women—the first to give an original and revolutionary view of women's past as defined by gender and role. Important reading for all women who are interested in the origin of their position in society today.

Bachofen, J. J. *Myth, Religion, & Mother Right.* Princeton: Princeton University Press, 1967. A selection of the writings of J. J. Bachofen, translated from the German by Ralph Manheim. An examination of ancient symbol and myth, and the development of the author's theory of matriarchy, of "mother right."

Becker, Ernest. *The Denial of Death.* New York: Macmillan Publishing Co., Ltd., 1973. Becker tries in this book to show that the fear of death is universal, and how clear and intelligible human actions are that we have buried under fact, and what we call "true" human motives.

Belenky, Mary Field, and Blythe McVicker Clinchy, Nancy Rule Goldberger, Jill Mattuck Tarule. *Women's Way of Knowing.* New York: Basic Books, Inc., 1986. Models of human learning are based on male experience, in which men use the sense of sight to establish a subject-object relationship with the world. This book studies how women view reality and draw conclusions about truth, knowledge, and authority, and how they use hearing to establish connections with the world.

Bly, Robert. *Iron John: A Book About Men.* Reading, MA: Addison-Wesley Publishing Company, Inc., 1990. Bly uses the myth of the Grimm brothers' "Iron Man" to shape a new vision of adult manhood from a very ancient one.

Bodian. Stephen, ed. "Being Intimate." *Yoga Journal* (May/June 1987). A survey of contemporary views of relationship. Although containing useful practical suggestions, these views are not necessarily yogic.

Bolen, Jean Shinoda. *Goddesses in Everywoman: A New Psychology of Women.* New York: Harper & Row, 1985. An introduction to the patterns of cultural stereotypes of women, in the guise of seven archetypal goddesses, or personality types, with whom all women can identify.

Boswell, John. *The Kindness of Strangers: The Abandonment of Children in Western Europe from Late Antiquity to the Renaissance.* New York: Pantheon Books, 1988. The ancient and medieval abandonment of children was a widespread and familiar part of domestic life in most of Europe, a custom regulated by the Church and civil authorities, and often essential to the survival of the family.

Bridges, William. *Transitions: Making Sense of Life's Changes.* Reading, MA: Addison-Wesley Publishing Company, 1980. Bridges helps both in identifying and in coping with critical changes in life, examining the underlying pattern of transition, whatever the specific change.

Brown, Cheever MacKenzie. *God as Mother.* Hartford, VT: Claude Stark & Co., 1974. A feminine theology with an appreciation for Divine Mother as well as Father. Devotion of this kind provides balance for this age of spiritual search and social justice, and brings a new sense of respect for womanhood.

Brown, Gabrielle. *The New Celibacy.* New York: Ballantine Books, 1980. Why more men and women are abstaining from sex—and enjoying it. A period of celibacy is a way of breaking boundaries—old patterns of behavior that exist between the mind and body, between the self and others. It enables one to be free of sexuality in order to evaluate and experience the joys of life without sex.

Brown, Peter. *The Body and Society: Men, Women, and Sexual Renunciation in Early Christianity*. New York: Columbia University Press, 1988. This book studies sexual renunciation among the early Christians, from Paul to Augustine, outlining the diversity of such practices as well as the growth of asceticism, and of the view of sex as sin.

Bumiller, Elisabeth. *May You Be the Mother of a Hundred Sons*. New York: Random House, 1990. A unique word picture of the paradoxes and realities of the lives of Indian women. Bumiller talked with Indian women in all walks of life, and the result is a book that raises vital questions for women around the world.

Chesler, Phyllis. *About Men*. New York: Simon and Shuster, 1978. Chesler explores men's relationships between fathers and sons, men and women, and between each other. As she says, she writes "in the belief that understanding can weaken the worship of death—that has dominated patriarchal consciousness and human action for so long."

Coleman, Arthur, and Libby Coleman. *The Father: Mythology and Changing Roles*. Wilmette, IL: Chiron Publications, 1988. This book examines the changing role of the father in today's family, and explores the impact of fatherhood on a man's life.

Combs-Schilling, M. E. *Sacred Performances: Islam, Sexuality, and Sacrifice*. New York: Columbia University Press, 1989. The Eastern cultures have a unique view of the saying that God created the earth, and told humankind to conquer it and multiply. In the Orient a man sees a woman as a means to multiply himself, and feels his manhood is established by spilling blood, that is by turning woman from a virgin into a life-giving vessel.

Corneau, Guy. *Absent Fathers, Lost Sons: The Search for Masculine Identity*. London: Shambhala, 1991. Men, says Corneau, live in a "hereditary silence" that denies every boy's need for recognition or confirmation from his father. Men must break out of this silence to bridge the gap between "the abstract, disincarnated minds of men and an increasingly cruel world."

Daly, Mary. *Beyond God the Father: Toward a Philosophy of Women's Liberation*. Boston: Beacon Press, 1974. Daly explores the importance for women to reclaim their right to name, and to use symbols in a different, feminine way. With the liberation of language, she sees the possibility of the liberation of humanity.

———. *Gyn/Ecology: The Metaethics of Radical Feminism*. Boston: Beacon Press, 1978. A story of transformation that is "both discovery and creation of a world other than patriarchy."

Davis, Elizabeth Gould. *The First Sex*. New York: Penguin Books Inc., 1975. Drawing on science, mythology, archeology, and history, the author aims to give woman her rightful place in history, and to prove that woman's contribution to civilization has been greater than man's.

de Beauvoir, Simone. *The Second Sex*. Toronto: Bantam Books, 1970. A total picture of what de Beauvoir has learned, observed, and thought from her exploration of the sexual, social, biological, and historical aspects of femininity.

Diner, Helen. *Mothers and Amazons*. New York: The Julian Press, Inc., 1965. The first feminine history of culture. This work is based on the writings of Bachofen, Jung, and Freud, supplemented by a study of ancient source materials. It tells the story of female-dominated societies that existed in earlier civilizations, and dispels the idea of male superiority. It also shows that under matriarchies there were virtually no sexual inhibitions and almost no sexual jealousy.

Doresse, Jean. *The Secret Books of the Egyptian Gnostics*. New York: Viking Press, 1960. Doresse was largely responsible for bringing to light the early Christian mystical traditions that had been recorded by the Egyptian Gnostics.

Dworkin, Andrea. *Right-Wing Women*. New York: G. P. Putman's Sons, 1983. Dworkin believes that fear of violence pervades women's relationships with men. She explains how this leads some women to become anti-abortionists, and led to the defeat the Equal Rights Amendment in the U.S.

Ehrenreich, Barbara. *The Hearts of Men: American Dreams and the Flight from Commitment*. Garden City, NY: Anchor Books, 1984. Ehrenreich looks at the male revolt against the breadwinner ethic and explores the question of "whether the rebels of both sexes have enough in common to work together toward a more generous, dignified and caring society."

Eliade, Mircea. *Yoga: Immortality and Freedom*. New York: Pantheon Books Inc., 1958. An exhaustive study of the tradition of Yoga, and a reconstruction of the history of the most important ascetic techniques of India. It provides a comprehensive background for yogic thought and practices.

Fasteau, Marc Feigen. *The Male Machine.* New York: Dell Publishing Co., Inc., 1975. A myth-shattering book about men—their sexuality, and their relationships with each other and with women. This often painful inquiry into the male condition complements the feminist revolution.

Fisher, Helen E. *The Sex Contract: The Evolution of Human Behavior.* New York: William Morrow and Company, Inc., 1982. This presentation shows how an upright stance created radical changes in human sexuality, and gives a balanced and harmonious view of the important roles played by women, men, and children in the course of human evolution.

Francoeur, Robert T. *Utopian Motherhood: New Trends in Human Reproduction.* Cranbury, NJ: A. S. Barnes and Co., Inc., 1977. This book outlines the choice between the development of wisdom to participate in the ongoing creation of human beings, and the possibility of creating "asexual assembly—produced, thought-controlled, genetically engineered ghosts" of men and women. As the author points out, "we do not yet know what it means to be male or female in this brave new world of ours."

Freund, Philip. *Myths of Creation.* Levittown, NY: Transatlantic Arts, Inc., 1975. An exploration of the human mind through the creation myths of other religions and races.

Frith, Nigel. *The Legend of Krishna.* New York: Shocken Books, 1976. A very readable book that tells the story of Krishna through the various stages of his life, with the intent of giving the reader the flavor of the experience of this important Indian god.

Fromm, Erich. *The Art of Loving.* New York: Harper & Brothers, 1956. Fromm's book on the many facets of love is still applicable today. His statement that "love is the only sane and satisfactory answer to the problem of human existence" has no limits of time.

Garrison, Omar. *Tantra: The Yoga of Sex.* New York: The Julian Press, Inc., 1964. The understanding of sex, its powers, and possible development to other levels is very well and clearly presented in this book.

Gilligan, Carol. *In a Different Voice.* Cambridge: Harvard University Press, 1982. An important contribution to the understanding of moral development in both men and women. One of the voices proclaiming the need for a psychology of women that does not treat them as if they were men.

Gilmore, David D. *Manhood in the Making: Cultural Concepts of Masculinity.* New York: Yale University Press, 1991. The first cross-cultural study of manhood as an achieved status finds that a culturally sanctioned stress on manliness—on toughness and aggressiveness, stoicism and sexuality—is almost universal.

Goldberg, Herb. *The Hazards of Being Male: Surviving the Myth of Masculine Privilege.* New York: The New American Library, 1976. A liberating approach to maleness that exposes the myth of masculine privilege and power.

Goergen, Donald. *The Sexual Celibate.* New York: Image Books, 1979. Goergen has approached this subject in the context of both the theology and psychology of sexuality. The importance of sexuality and celibacy is the degree in which each contributes to the humanization and spiritualization of individuals.

Graves, Robert. *The White Goddess: A Historical Grammar of Poetic Myth.* New York: Farrar, Straus and Giroux, 1980. The thesis of this book is that "the language of poetic myth anciently current in the Mediterranean and Northern Europe was a magical language bound up with popular religious ceremonies in honor of the Moon-goddess, or Muse, some of them dating from the Old Stone Age, and that this remains the language of true poetry—'true' in the nostalgic modern sense of 'the unimprovable original, not a synthetic substitute.'" The book is a history of the problem of service to the Goddess.

Guenther, Herbert V. *The Tantric View of Life.* Berkeley: Shambhala Publications, Inc., 1972. Guenther offers a major contribution toward understanding the meaning of Tantra, which is clearly defined. The philosophy and practice of Tantra is presented in depth, and light is shed on human sexuality, its dilemma and validity.

Guillaumont, A., trans. *The Gospel According to Thomas: Coptic Text Established and Translated.* New York: Harper & Row, 1959. The remains of an extraordinary Coptic library, lost for sixteen centuries and discovered in 1945 in a ruined tomb near Nag Hammadi, Upper Egypt, has yielded an extensive collection of 114 "sayings of Jesus." These are open to consideration as possibly containing genuine words of Jesus heretofore unknown.

Gustafson, Janie. *Celibate Passion.* San Francisco: Harper & Row, 1978. The contradiction and paradox of our thirst for union with another, yet hunger to be singular and unique, can lead to transformation and inner renewal.

Haich, Elisabeth. *Sexual Energy and Yoga.* New York: ASI Publishers Inc., 1972. Excellent resource material on the transmutation of sexual energy, using Eastern and Western symbolism.

Harding, M. Esther. *Woman's Mysteries: Ancient and Modern.* New York: Harper & Row, 1976. A psychological interpretation of the feminine principle as portrayed in myth, story, and dreams. Myths of ancient times and primitive peoples reflect in the inner states of mind and attitudes of women and men from all ages. The inner subjective conflicts must be resolved before the problem of external conflict, including misunderstandings between men and women, can be solved.

———. *The Way of All Women: A Psychological Interpretation.* New York: G. P. Putnam's Sons for the C. G. Jung Foundation for Analytical Psychology, 1970. In her introduction Harding notes that "man creates the idea and woman transforms it into a living reality." She use psychological theory to demonstrate a method of living, which makes this book as relevant today, for both men and women, as when it was written.

Hapgood, Fred. *Why Males Exist.* New York: New American Library, 1979. A very readable exploration of the purpose of males (since they are dependent on female desires for survival), why a separate male sex developed, and why human beings are not bisexual (because that kind of reproduction works very well).

Hawley, John Stratton. *Krishna, the Butter Thief.* Princeton: Princeton University Press, 1983. Hawley shows how Krishna's role as butter thief is connected with him as the irresistible lover. Both illustrate the intimate relation that Hindus see between God and humanity.

Hawley, John Stratton, and Donna Marie Wulff, ed. *The Divine Consort: Radha and the Goddesses of India.* Boston: Beacon Press, 1986. A glimpse of the Indian religion and culture through an exploration of the history and legacy of goddesses, particularly Radha, in an overwhelmingly patriarchal society.

Heilbrun, Carolyn G. *Toward a Recognition of Androgyny.* New York: Harper & Row, Harper Colophon Books, 1974. A stimulating search into myth and literature to trace manifestations of androgyny—woman-in-man, man-in-woman—and to reveal the dangers of sexual polarization.

Hite, Shere. *Women and Love.* New York: Alfred A. Knopf, 1987. A revelation of how the women in America really feel about their relationships with the men in their lives.

Johnson, Robert. *He.* Revised Edition. New York: Harper Perennial, 1989. Explores the Grail myth in terms of masculine psychology.

————. *Transformation: Understanding the Three Levels of Masculine Consciousness.* San Francisco: Harper, 1991. Using the figures of Don Quixote, Hamlet, and Faust from classical literature, Johnson has demonstrated the stages of personal growth by which men can achieve maturity and wholeness.

Jung, C. G. *Aspects of the Masculine.* Translated by R. F. C. Hull. Princeton: Princeton Bollingen Paperback, 1989. A collection of Jung's most important contributions to the psychological understanding of masculinity in both sexes. Included are some far-ranging observations on the differences between men's and women's psychology.

Kakar, Sudhir. *The Inner World.* Delhi: Oxford University Press, 1981. A psychoanalytic study of childhood and society in India. A description of the effect of religious ideals and historical traditions on human development within the Indian culture.

Karlsan, Carol F. *The Devil in the Shape of a Woman: Witchcraft in Colonial New England.* New York: W. W. Norton & Company, 1987. By focusing on witchcraft in a particular setting and at a specific time, Karlsan has addressed ideas about women, fears about women, and the general place of women in society.

Keen, Sam. *Fire in the Belly: On Being a Man.* New York: Bantam Books, 1991. This book examines key male issues from the point of view of popular psychology and the author's personal experience.

Kinsley, David R. *The Sword and the Flute: Kali and Krsna, Dark Visions of the Terrible and the Sublime in Hindu Mythology.* Berkeley: University of California Press, 1975. A study of the underlying visions and central truths of the Hindu religious tradition, shown through an investigation of Krishna as the Divine Child and as the Divine Lover.

Krishna, Gopi. *Kundalini: The Evolutionary Energy in Man.* Berkeley: Shambhala Publications, 1972. This is an autobiographical account of what happens to the mind and body when Kundalini is aroused spontaneously, and it describes the traditional Hindu theories about this force.

Laquer, Thomas. *Making Sex: Body and Gender from the Greeks to Freud.* Cambridge: Harvard University Press, n.d. This book presents a simple theme—that sex is so important in itself, and that it is a sign, symbol, or reflection of nearly everything in our culture—with clarity and with broad implications.

Leonard, Linda Schierse. *The Wounded Woman: Healing the Father-Daughter*

Relationship. Boston: Shambhala, 1983. Leonard shows that by understanding the father-daughter wound and working to transform it psychologically, it is possible to achieve a relationship between the sexes that honors both the mutuality and the uniqueness of each.

Lerner, Gerder. *The Creation of Patriarchy*. New York: Oxford University Press, 1986. Lerner suggests that instead of searching for matriarchy, because it is so nebulous, to search for the beginnings of patriarchy, to look at the beginnings of women's subordination, and the way they have contributed to it throughout history. What has a beginning can have an end.

Margulis, Lynn, and Dorion Sagan. *Mystery Dance: On the Evolution of Human Sexuality*. New York: Summit Books, 1992. Tracing human sexuality back through primates, hominids, reptiles, aquatic life, and finally to the bacteria that were earth's original life form, it can be seen that our sexual behavior incorporates strong instinctual remnants of all our ancestors. This book demonstrates to the yogic reader the strength of instinct.

Mead, Margaret. *Male and Female*. New York: Dell Publishing Co., Inc., 1973. A long-standing contribution to the understanding of our own culture arising from the author's studies of the sexual behavior in many cultures.

———. *Sex and Temperament in Three Primitive Societies*. New York: The New American Library, 1950. Mead challenges us to re-examine our social structure as she traces the shaping of men and women to the pattern of temperament and behavior that each society has assigned to them.

Mehra, Parmanand S. *Shrimat Bhagwat Gita in Pictures [Bhagavad Gita]*. Bombay: Parmanand Publications., circ. 1953. A beautifully illustrated retelling of Krishna's teachings to Arjuna on the meaning of life and Yoga.

Miller, Alice. *Prisoners of Childhood: The Drama of the Gifted Child and the Search for the True Self*. New York: Basic Books, Inc., 1981. Illustrating clearly what can happen when children are not regarded as spiritual gifts, Miller describes the process by which children mirror their parents' image of them in order to be accepted, and so grow up never knowing their true selves.

———. *For Your Own Good: Hidden Cruelty in Child-Rearing and the Roots of Violence*. New York: Farrar, Straus, Giroux, 1983. Hitler, says Miller, was a natural outcome of the child-rearing practices prevalent in Western society for hundreds of years, in which all children are used to a greater or lesser degree to gratify their parents' emotional needs.

———. *Thou Shalt Not Be Aware: Society's Betrayal of the Child*. New York:

Farrar, Straus, Giroux, 1985. Society justifies the maltreatment of children by universally placing the blame on the victim and protecting the parent. Miller suggests all children should be treated as Mary and Joseph treated Jesus: as a gift from God.

Miller, Patrick. "Journey of the Heart." *Yoga Journal* (March/April 1991). A survey of contemporary views on relationship from writings of and interviews with Stephen and Ondrea Levine, John Welwood, and Gay and Kathryn Hendricks. These views are not necessarily yogic, though many of the suggestions are useful and practical.

Miller, Jean Baker. *Toward a New Psychology of Women.* Boston: Beacon Press, 1976. Baker was one of the first to document the effects of women's subordinate position on their psychological development—how and why it differs from men's and how this has been used to enforce inferiority.

Mollenkott, Virginia Ramey. *The Divine Feminine: The Biblical Imagery of God as Female.* New York: Crossroad, 1983. It is important to reclaim the biblical images of God as female to protect us from the stereotype of God as literally masculine.

Mookerjee, Ajit. *Kali: The Feminine Force.* New York: Destiny Books, 1988. Using the powerful imagery of paintings, sculptures, and writings, this celebration of Kali explores and illumines the rich meanings of feminine divinity.

Moore, Charles A., ed., with the assistance of Aldyth V. Morris. *The Indian Mind: Essentials of Indian Philosophy and Culture.* Honolulu: East-West Center Press, University of Hawaii Press, 1967. A series of essays presenting a middle-of-the-road explanation of the Indian mind as expressed through its philosophies, religions, and social thought and practices.

Noddings, Nel. *Women and Evil.* Berkeley: University of California Press, 1989. Evil is real, and people must find a way to face and overcome it. The book is an attempt to describe a morality of evil.

Ochs, Carol. *Behind the Sex of God: Toward a New Consciousness—Transcending Matriarchy and Patriarchy.* Boston: Beacon Press, 1977. The opposition of matriarchy and patriarchy in religious thought extends into the lives of men and women. Considering a third mode of thought—androgyny—is also an attempt to reconcile the sexes.

O'Flaherty, Wendy Doniger. *Asceticism and Eroticism in the Mythology of Siva.* London: Oxford University Press, 1973. The development of an Indian approach to the continuing conflict between spiritual aspirations and human desires.

———. *Hindu Myths*. Markham, ON: Penguin Group, 1982. The traditional Hindu themes of life and death are set forth in this book, and interwoven with many complex variations, which give a kaleidoscopic picture of the development of almost 3,000 years of Indian mythology.

———. *The Origins of Evil in Hindu Mythology*. Berkeley: University of California Press, 1976. An excellent study covering sex symbols, the worship of the shivalinga, the meaning of the serpent or snake in its negative aspects, and the question of evil. This topic is in contrast to the Serpent Power or Kundalini, which is a divine manifestation.

Osherson, Samuel. *Finding our Fathers: How a Man's Life is Shaped by His Father*. New York: Fawcett Columbine, 1986. Osherman penetrates the shroud of silence that surrounds the deepest feelings and fears of men. He shows how they can resolve the inner conflict of the father-son relationship that contributes to problems in family life and career.

Ostheimer, Nancy C., and John M. Ostheimer, eds. *Life or Death: Who Controls?* New York: Springer Publishing Company, Inc., 1976. Articles on eugenics, abortion, sterilization, and euthanasia have been brought together and edited by Nancy and John Ostheimer. Together they make up a thought-provoking book that brings into question the ethical basis of modern practices, and possibilities for the future.

Pagels, Elaine. *Adam, Eve, and the Serpent*. New York: Random House, Inc., 1988. An exploration of the attitudes that Jesus and his followers took toward human nature, including marriage, family, procreation, and celibacy. This book gives an opportunity to look into the attitudes regarding sexuality and marriage that we in the West have come to take for granted.

Parrinder, Geoffrey. *Sex in the World's Religions*. New York: Oxford University Press, 1980. A useful view of the place of sex in various religions. It includes examinations of marriage, celibacy, love, and yoga, as well as mystical union and symbolism.

Patai, Raphael. *The Hebrew Goddess*. New York: Avon Books, 1978. Patai's central thesis is that Hebrew and Jewish religion, rather than being a consistently paternalistic monotheistic faith, at many periods was not only tinged with polytheism, but centered on the veneration of a goddess who appeared by many names.

Powell, Marilyn. "The World According to Women." Toronto: Canadian

Broadcasting Corporation, 1991. Transcript of a radio series. Influential women thinkers, including Marilyn French, Carol Gilligan, Margaret Attwood, Germaine Greer, Erica Jong, and others, talk about patriarchy, power, politics, and violence.

Rank, Otto. *Beyond Psychology.* New York: Dover Publications, 1958. An exploration of the institution of marriage, power and the state, the creation of the sexual self, feminine psychology and masculine ideology, and psychology beyond the self.

Ranke-Heinemann, Uta. *Eunuchs for the Kingdom of Heaven: Women, Sexuality, and the Catholic Church.* Translated by Peter Heinogg. New York: Doubleday, 1990. The Church has denigrated sex, degraded women, and championed a perverse ideal of celibacy, and has played a fateful role in shaping the sexual behavior of the Western world.

Rawson, Philip. *The Art of Tantra.* New York: Oxford University Press, 1978. Through text and illustrations, this book demonstrates a personal meditative and visual exploration of self and the world.

Roerich, George N. *The Blue Annals.* Delhi: Motilal Banarsidass, 1979. This work establishes a firm chronology of events in Tibetan history, and gives the names of famous religious teachers and their spiritual lineage. The fifteen chapters are each dedicated to the history of a particular school or sect of Tibetan Buddhism.

Rorvik, David. *In His Image: The Cloning of a Man.* Philadelphia: J. B. Lippincott Company, 1978. The intriguing account of a doctor willing to risk the controversial procedure of creating a human genetic "twin" by cloning, and the moral problems that arose as a result of such experimentation with human life.

Saradananda, Swami. *Sri Ramakrishna: The Great Master.* Myalpore, India: Sri Ramakrishna Math, 1952. A detailed account of the life of a unique personality, combining a record of events and a history of the mind of this great man.

Scanzoni, John. *Sexual Bargaining: Power Politics in the American Marriage.* Chicago: The University of Chicago Press, 1972. The evolution of modern marriage through the "reward seeking" that generates conflict between men and women. This book explores the changes that are taking place in equality of the sexes, both within and outside marriage, and their effects on the institution of marriage.

Shastri, Hari Prasad, trans. *Narada Sutras: The Philosophy of Love.* London:

Shanti Sadan, 1963. The sage Narada explains the nature of devotion in a series of aphorisms *(sutras)* that, although of great antiquity, are still applicable to modern life.

Sheehy, Gail. *Passages: Predictable Crises of Adult Life.* New York: E. P. Dutton & Co., Inc., 1976. *Passages* shows the pattern of adult developmental stages, and compares the rhythms in development of men and women, which Sheehy found to be strikingly different.

Siddiqi, M. Mazheruddin. *Women in Islam.* New Delhi: Adam Publishers, 1980. An exploration of how Islamic injunctions in the regulation of sex and family life can be adapted to modern life without departing from Muslim principles.

Singer, Milton, ed. *Krishna, Myths, Rites, and Attitudes.* Chicago: The University of Chicago Press, 1966. A collection of studies of the legends of Krishna as divine child and divine lover.

Sinh, Pancham, trans. *The Hatha Yoga Pradipika,* 3d ed. New Delhi: Munshiram Manoharlal Publishers, 1980. This is an important text that contains the essentials of Yoga. As well as describing the stages and correct methods for the practice of Yoga, it also discusses the underlying philosophy.

Stone, Merlin. *When God Was a Woman.* New York: Harcourt Brace Jovanovich, 1978. Here, archaeologically documented, is the story of the religion of the Goddess, revered as the wise creator and the one source of universal order. The patriarchal re-imaging of the Goddess took place through the rewriting of myth and religious dogmas.

Sovatsky, Stanley. "The Pleasures of Celibacy." *Yoga Journal* (March/April 1987). A succinct explanation of aspects of the experience of *brahmacharya.*

Tannen, Deborah. *You Just Don't Understand.* New York: William Morrow and Company, Inc., 1990. This book offers a "totally new approach to a peace treaty in the battle between the sexes at work or home," and shows the source of many of the difficulties between men and women, which begin in the early stages of life.

Tharchin, Sermey Geshe Lobsang. *King Udrayana and the Wheel of Life.* Howell, NJ: The Mahayana and Sutra Press, 1984. The Wheel of Life, with its depiction of the beings of the world caught in the grasp of Death, is a traditional painting familiar to every student of Tibetan Buddhist art. This work presents the wonderful events leading to its creation, the fact that it was designed by the Buddha himself, and the precise meaning of the Wheel.

Tyberg, Judith M. *The Language of the Gods: Sanskrit Keys to India's Wisdom.* Los Angeles: East-West Cultural Center, 1970. This book is not just an introduction to the Sanskrit language, but is also a very good introduction to the literature and spiritual teachings of the religion of India.

von Urban, Rudolf. *Sex Perfection and Marital Happiness.* New York: The Dial Press, Inc., 1949. After receiving his M.D. from the University of Vienna, von Urban studied psychology, psychiatry, and sexology for many years. In this book he explains the nuances of the sex relation in all its phases, in an effort to make possible the sex perfection that he claims is the natural right of every adult human being.

Walker, Lenore E. *The Battered Woman.* New York: Harper Colophon, 1979. Walker has written a thorough, practical, compassionate, and authoritative examination of the problem of battered women, which is more pervasive than it was ever thought to be, and the myths that have rationalized such behavior.

Watts, Alan W. *Nature, Man and Woman.* New York: Vantage Books, 1970. The alienation and loneliness in the Western relationship between human beings and nature is discussed. Watts shows the origins of this alienation in Christianity, and explores the means of overcoming it through changing attitudes to both nature and the expression of love between a man and a woman.

Wilber, Ken. "Sex, Gender, and Transcendence." *The Quest* (Summer 1991). Alter, Wendy. "Letters to the Editor." *The Quest* (Winter 1991). A discussion of the origin, effects, and meaning, if any, of the double standard.

Wilson, Edward O. *On Human Nature.* Cambridge: Harvard University Press, 1978. Wilson shows the traces evolution has left on human activities, how the origin of the patterns of generosity, self-sacrifice, and worship, as well as sexuality and aggression, are revealed in the life histories of primate bands that hunted big game in the last Ice Age. He also shows that a misunderstanding of biological fact is the basis of discrimination against ethnic groups, homosexuals, and women.

Wilson, H. H., trans. *The Visnu Puranas.* Delhi: Nag Publishers, 1980.

Wood, Ernest E. *Practical Yoga: Ancient and Modern.* Hollywood: Wilshire Book Company, 1972. This is a translation of Patanjali's *Yoga Aphorisms,* interpreted in the light of ancient and modern psychological knowledge and practical experience. For the modern Western reader it provides a useful explanation of this traditional system of yoga.

Woodroffe, Sir. J. *Shakti and Shakta*. London: Luzac, 1929.

Woolf, Naomi. *The Beauty Myth*. Toronto: Vintage Books, 1991. Far from seeing the body as a miracle or a spiritual tool, many women are abusing their bodies in the attempt to achieve an artificial and damaging standard of beauty. Woolf details the self-destructive extent to which many are prepared to go in the search for illusory acceptance.

Index